Changing the Mind
Healing the Body

Changing the Mind
Healing the Body

Eight Case Studies in
Transformational Belief-Change
Therapy

Elly Roselle
as told to A.S.A. Harrison

Ugly Duckling Editions
Toronto, Canada

First Ugly Duckling Edition, 2005

Library and Archives Canada Cataloguing in Publication

Roselle, Elly, 1948–
    Changing the mind, healing the body : eight case studies in transformational belief-change therapy / Elly Roselle ; as told to A.S.A. Harrison.

ISBN 0-9738175-0-X

    1. Mental healing—Case studies. 2. Sick—Psychology—Case studies.
I. Harrison, A.S.A. II. Title.

RZ401.R67 2005   615.8'51
C2005-902882-3

TO ORDER:
www.uglyducklingeditions.info

TO CONTACT THE PUBLISHER:
ask@uglyducklingeditions.info

Author photo page 229 by Brian Giebelhaus
Set in 10 point Book Antiqua
Printed in Canada

Contents

Foreword

In *Changing the Mind, Healing the Body* Elly Roselle approaches symptoms and diseases not as enemies to be fought and defeated but as messages from the self that need to be decoded, their meanings to be taken to heart. At the core of her transformational belief-change therapy is the conviction that our lifelong unconscious belief systems — acquired in childhood — influence our internal physiological milieu, either for illness or for health. Her technique consists of a skillful and compassionate probing of her clients' hidden mind states as they are related to their various organs or to symptoms arising from those organs.

Roselle accepts and works with the mind/body unity and in this she is on solid scientific ground. This unity is no longer to be doubted by anyone familiar with the new science of psychoneuroimmunology and with the many thousands of research papers published in the past several decades showing the interactions of the immune centers, the brain, the nervous system and the hormonal apparatus.

As a scientifically trained doctor of orthodox Western medicine, I would not wish to endorse Roselle's work as "the" answer to illness — nor would she expect or demand such recognition. Her claims for successful healing are never ostentatious or self-serving — she has the humility not to ascribe cures or improvements to her work alone. What I can say is that her fundamental approach is one I am in sympathy with, that her case studies strike me as entirely credible, and that her insights —

or more correctly, the insights she helps people gain about themselves — are both startling and inspiring. The outcomes for patients include increased physical well being and psychological peace. Inner conflict, the body fighting itself or struggling to teach itself painful but necessary lessons, is greatly reduced.

The result, as one patient points out, is integration: a sense of becoming whole. And to become whole, it so happens, is also the root meaning of the word heal.

Gabor Maté, MD
Author of *When the Body Says No*

Preface

Some years ago, on becoming acquainted with Elly Roselle and her methods, I was inspired to approach her about working together on this book. We began by reviewing her cases and obtaining permission from those whose stories we wanted to use. Fortunately, Roselle had made and kept audio recordings of her sessions with clients, in addition to handwritten notes. I transcribed the audio, reviewed the notes and mapped out the narratives. We then followed up with many hours of consultation to make refinements and add Roselle's commentary. In all cases we have changed identifying details to protect the privacy of those involved.

It's been a great privilege to have a hand in shaping these remarkable documents. A subtle alchemy happens in Roselle's therapy sessions — an alchemy that takes place entirely within the inner space of the subject. Mind/body links become tangible; subconscious contents come to life; psychic spaces transform; and the conscious mind, which always remains in charge of proceedings, grows stronger and clearer.

It is my hope that readers will gain insight and understanding from these case studies, which offer new perspectives on the nature and origin of physical illness.

A.S.A. Harrison

Introduction

The case studies in this book are drawn from my private practice as a psychotherapist. They illustrate an innovative approach to healing—a way of working with the mind to find and resolve the psychological components of physical disease. They also offer a contemporary vision of therapy, one that draws on Western models while recognizing that mind and body are indivisible.

The mind/body connection has been the subject of widespread discussion in recent years and there is much intriguing evidence in its support, some scientific and some anecdotal. In the anecdotal category one particular story seems to crop up again and again: that people with Dissociative Identity Disorder (formerly known as Multiple Personality Disorder) have been found to suffer from certain physical symptoms in one personality and yet not in another. I find this easily credible and mention it here because it illustrates two of my basic precepts: that our personalities (beliefs, attitudes, coping strategies) play a major role in fostering and maintaining physical ailments; and that our bodies are far more responsive and changeable than is generally believed.

I present here the stories of seven people who elicited my help with healing. Their ailments range from potentially deadly conditions (cancer, HIV) to debilitating chronic complaints (allergies, hypothyroidism, myalgic encephalomyelitis, vaginismus) to eating disorders (bulimia, sugar addiction). All of them sought me out after the medical profession had failed to help them. In some instances my work took place concurrent with medical treatment.

My services are not a substitute for medicine.

Each story illustrates my techniques in detail and also provides an intimate view of the evolution and logic of an illness from a mental/emotional perspective. The cases are graphic and reveal the subtle mechanics of mind/body interactions. They also offer new and surprising perspectives on the origin and nature of disease.

My specific methodology is built on two decades of independent study and experimental work with clients. Its seeds were planted long ago—when I was a child of fourteen and came across a book on Freud in the school library. Much of the text was beyond my comprehension but I was impressed by one central concept: When people develop "complexes" they're stuck with them for the rest of their lives; the best they can do, even after years of analysis, is get better at coping. I felt extremely crestfallen when I read this. Not really knowing who Freud was, I put the book down and decided not to pick it up again. Ironically, that same year I developed the anorexia and bulimia that were to plague me for the next twenty years, making me an excellent case in point for Dr. Freud.

By the time I reached my twenties I had spent many hours with analytic psychiatrists. I'd had bad reactions to the drugs they prescribed and had come to realize that they did not have the tools to heal my eating disorder. Meanwhile, however, my search for a cure had deepened my interest in psychology and its links to the body. I began to study contemporary therapies, such as Feldenkrais, Gestalt, Eriksonian hypnotherapy and the work of Virginia Satir. In my early thirties I spent time thinking through and trying out new techniques. One day, a single experiment effected a complete and permanent resolution of my anorexia and bulimia (see "Epilogue").

This experience had a significant impact on my goals and direction as a therapist. I saw that not only was it possible to effect change at a deep, fundamental level of the self, but that it did not necessarily require years of daily or weekly counseling sessions.

Observing that my cure had come about through the transformation of a core belief, I continued my investigations along these lines. I was rewarded with evidence that others were also helped when they made belief changes, regardless of their presenting problem. As I consolidated my approach I gave it a name, Core Belief Engineering, which reflects my project of modifying or transforming the fundamental premises that build our lives.

My ideas and methods are fully illustrated in these pages. Some of my precepts will be familiar to professionals, yet I know of no other therapy in which they are so effectively harnessed to techniques for transformation. My approach fits loosely into the school that identifies belief as the main psychological factor influencing behavior. I am by no means the first to observe that our beliefs shape our attitudes, perceptions and interactions, profoundly affecting our life experience. The Austrian psychiatrist Alfred Adler (1870-1937) wrote extensively on the importance of beliefs. Adler said that, as children, our experiences lead us to form convictions about ourselves, others and the world—but because our reasoning faculties have not yet developed, our convictions are often fictions or partial truths. (I am worthless; people are mean; life is hard.) Such biased perceptions form the personal mythology or cognitive map that carries us into adulthood.

While the idea that beliefs structure experience has gained acceptance, my work is unique and specific in its tools for identifying and transforming those beliefs. At the base of my approach is a picture of the subconscious mind as a constellation of "parts." We are all familiar with the phenomenon of autonomous subpersonalities as it occurs in Dissociative Identity Disorder, but less attention has been paid to the natural compartmentalization of the psyche that we all live with. We speak of this intuitively when we say things like: "Part of me wants to lose weight but another part of me loves to eat." Fritz Perls worked with the phenomenon of parts in his Gestalt approach to therapy, and Virginia Satir pioneered her living-theatre model as a way of negotiating with parts.

In my view such parts are actual components of the subconscious — somewhat like children living within us. In my working model each part has a distinct identity that incorporates a picture of reality, a survival urge, a job to do, a style of expression, a strategy, feelings, talents and a personal history based on its own selective memory. Each part also has a unique set of beliefs and a characteristic way of linking to the physiology. Some of our parts are unknown to us while others move in and out of conscious awareness. In sessions, I ask clients to communicate directly with their parts — an unusual thing to ask, and yet most people do it easily. It's normal to engage with our inner workings — our thoughts, feelings, bodily sensations. Communicating more formally with these aspects of ourselves is simply an extension of what comes naturally.

Parts create problems in our lives because they tend to get stuck in automatic, repetitive behavior patterns. They often act against our current best interests or maintain habits against our will. Our parts are not out to get us but they may be out of touch and using coping strategies that are not very effective. Thus, the part that overeats might simply be trying to give us pleasure, having decided, for instance, that eating is the only safe or reliable way to get enjoyment in life. By updating and re-educating such a part we can bring it into alignment with the goals and perspectives that we currently hold at a conscious level, thus restoring to conscious mind its rightful role of leadership. It is interesting to note that we sometimes confuse conscious thought with the analytical process. While reasoning can be an aspect of the conscious faculty, true conscious mind goes beyond the patterned and predictable responses exhibited by parts, and strongly inclines towards growth, change and creative expression.

One key to working with parts is recognizing that they absorb and store the emotions of other people. A part's own inherent energy can be obscured by the feelings of parents, siblings and others who have been influential in our lives. When parts let go of these stored emotions (through a process I call a psychic-emotive release) their inner clarity is immeasurably enhanced.

My goal in therapy is to reconnect each part with an abiding sense of self. Every part provides a path to one's personal sense of a core identity. A part can find this source by following its memories back in time to its beginnings (subjectively speaking) — to a place where it feels free of acquired beliefs and attitudes. This is a deeper consciousness at the heart of being — I call it the rollover. Different parts find it in different places — in early childhood, in the womb, at conception or even before this lifetime. Some parts at the rollover find simple peace and happiness, while others discover a sublime awareness or unity. The most common feeling at the rollover is love.

The stories that follow show how techniques for releasing emotions, altering core beliefs and accessing innate feelings of love can generate healing. Readers will notice the intriguing process of mapping a part's beliefs, the changes that occur when a part bonds with conscious mind, and the gentle negotiations that allow a part to change its orientation to life. On average, my sessions last from four to six hours. I always try for complete resolution of at least some aspect of a problem within a single session.

These stories show the power of the mind to shape and transform personal reality, including the condition of the physical body. Above all, they reveal what mystics have always known, and what modern healers are beginning to accept — that each of us has an inner core of goodness and love that is timeless and infinite, and that we can draw on for strength, renewal, peace and healing. I know this to be true because I have seen it time and time again in my journeys into the mind.

Elly Roselle

Neverland

Of the many bulimics I have worked with, Pearl is by far the most memorable. Not only was she a veteran hardcore case with all the classic symptoms, the underlying structure of her disorder was remarkable in its anatomy. When she first approached me she was thirty years old and had been bulimic since the age of twenty-two. I knew only too well what she was going through since I myself had been anorexic and bulimic for twenty years. Pearl had a serious problem for which there was no reliable treatment.

We met on a spring evening at a lecture I was giving on the relationship between beliefs and personal reality. A notice in a local newspaper had caught her eye, but she didn't realize till she got there that the event was sponsored by a group of old-school spiritualists—the kind who hold séances and commune with spirits. (In those early days I accepted every invitation to speak that came my way.) No sooner had Pearl arrived than she was seized by the urge to escape. Slipping quietly out the door, she fled towards the bus stop—but didn't get far. What stopped her, she told me later, felt like a "big hand" that gripped her on the shoulder, turned her around and guided her back into the lecture hall.

During my talk Pearl stood out as someone who seemed anxious and edgy. While most people in the audience were concerned about how their beliefs might be impairing their ability to contact the spirit world, Pearl asked questions about compulsive behavior and self-esteem. I was not surprised when she took me aside afterwards and confided that she was bulimic. The psychiatrist she was seeing had not been able to help her, she said, and she was beginning to feel desperate.

The pattern of bulimia is binge eating followed by vomiting. A bulimic will typically consume a huge stomachful of food, and then succumb to the urge to get rid of it. Both phases of the behavior, the eating and the throwing up, are compulsive. Like anorexics, bulimics are operating with a fat phobia and tend to feel they are never thin enough, no matter how emaciated they become. Also like anorexics, they welcome additional ways of getting their weight down, which may include excessive physical exercise and the use of laxatives and diuretics. The resulting chronic malnutrition takes its toll, the most common symptoms being irregular menstrual periods, erosion of tooth enamel and poor resistance to infection. A small percentage of cases die, often from heart failure.

There has been much speculation as to the cause of such eating disorders. Some say they are ways for a person who feels power-less to gain control. Often blamed are fashion trends that promote a skinny adolescent look, though anorexia and bulimia existed in previous centuries when it was acceptable for women to be heavier. In my opinion, all such generalizations have questionable value. Yes, there may be a need for control, a lack of self-esteem or an obsession with body image, and yet these traits are common to the majority of women in our culture. My own experience tells me that no two cases are alike. Beneath the superficial behavior patterns, the deep structure of an eating disorder is unique to the individual.

The conventional treatment for anorexia and bulimia is notoriously unreliable. It generally involves nutritional and psychological counseling along with an imposed eating regimen, which may involve a reward system and may include force feeding. Some practitioners add love and physical holding to this basic formula. The problem is, these methods involve months or years of institutionalization. For patients, this can be unpleasant and inconvenient to say the least, and the old patterns tend to resurface when they leave the hospital or clinic.

Most recently, some medical researchers have suggested that anorexia and bulimia may have a genetic base, but I have my doubts that these researchers are distinguishing between hard-wired genetics and kitchen-table genetics. If a woman feels powerless, empty and inadequate, for example, there is a good chance she will pass these feelings on to her daughters. This over-laying process may persist for generations.

Anorexia and bulimia were prominent in the media during the early 1980s with the much-publicized death of the singer Karen Carpenter. Since then, girls have been getting the idea of starving themselves or throwing up from other girls, or from movies or magazines. Pearl, on the other hand, had not learned her habit from anyone. In fact, she had been bulimic for two full years before she even found out there was a name for it.

By the time Pearl and I got together, she was acutely aware that her eating disorder was running her life. Outside of her part-time job as a lifeguard, the cycle of gorging and purging was her primary occupation. As is true for most bulimics, once was not enough. Pearl followed the typical pattern of pigging out, throwing up and then starting over again. The number of times per day a bulimic will do this depends on how much money and energy she has: what she can afford to spend on food and at what point she reaches exhaustion. (Oddly enough, exhaustion equals satisfaction in this obsessive cycle.) Pearl also suffered from depression, mood swings and low self-esteem.

I showed her into my consulting room at eleven o'clock on a Friday morning. I rarely make more than one appointment a day and usually begin in the morning because my sessions are long by normal standards, lasting at least three or four hours, sometimes much longer. As she took off her jacket and sat down, I noticed how attractive she was, with her large eyes and oval face framed by dark hair, neatly clipped to shoulder length. She didn't appear to be emaciated but it was hard to tell since she hid herself in baggy clothes. I found out later that at five foot seven she weighed only ninety-five pounds.

While Pearl presented herself as someone who was positive and forward-looking, I soon realized that it wasn't enthusiasm I was seeing so much as a kind of brittle determination. She saw herself as a survivor, carrying on against heavy odds. Her cheerfulness had an edge to it, her jokes were self-deprecating — and underneath it all was a delicate, fragile quality. When she avoided my questions about her bulimic habits I didn't press her on the subject, knowing that most bulimics are embarrassed by the sordid details of their disorder. Not until years later did I learn that she was in the habit of throwing up into a plastic bag and then hiding the bag in an empty milk carton, which was easy to dispose of discreetly. This ensured that she never left telltale traces of vomit around the house, helping to keep her secret safe from her three roommates. Her psychiatrist and I were probably the only people in the world who knew of her problem.

When I asked her about family, she frowned and said that she'd grown up in a southern US town with parents who didn't get along. Probing a little, I discovered that her mother had been an alcoholic and was now institutionalized with mental problems. She mentioned a brother who had died. As our conversation progressed she began to open up, and was soon revealing some very disturbing thoughts.

"I never seem to do the right thing," she said more than once. "When I should do something I don't and when I shouldn't do something I do." She shook her head mournfully. "I screw up a lot — I don't know what's wrong with me."

"What makes you think you screw up?" I asked.

She gave me a puzzled look.

"What happens inside that makes you feel this way?"

After thinking for a moment, she said, "You know, I've always had this sense of a horrible nagging voice telling me all these things that are wrong with me."

"Whose voice is it?" I asked.

She shook her head. "It feels like some kind of monster."

The voice, she said, berated her from morning till night, never giving her a moment's peace. When I asked where it was coming from, she said that it seemed to hover just behind her left shoulder. Its ridicule had her so filled with self-doubt that she found it hard to take any initiative in her life. Yet, although it made her feel helpless and inept, she struggled valiantly to keep up her confidence.

"I'm not such a hopeless case," she said. "There are lots of things I do well."

But the next moment she shrugged meekly. "Well, maybe I do a few things well but they don't really amount to much."

I remarked on these two opposing viewpoints and asked her which one she identified with most.

"I don't know." She creased her brow. "I am good at some things but I haven't really done anything with my life."

Although I empathized with her struggle, I allowed her internal argument to escalate so that she could begin to see these two sides of herself at work. The more she defended herself, the nastier the so-called monster became. After a while I could almost feel its presence in the room.

I recognized the monster as a "part" of Pearl—a compartmentalized aspect of her own psyche with a specific agenda and strategy. While it is normal for us to have such parts, I could see that this one was badly out of touch with Pearl and unaware of the anxiety it was causing her. It seemed that my work for the session was cut out for me. Among other things, I would have to create some self-awareness in the part, put it in touch with Pearl's daily reality and try to bring it into alignment with her conscious mind.

I began by asking Pearl if she would like to have a talk with the monster.

She looked at me blankly.

"Would you be curious to know more about it? I wonder if it has something to offer besides criticism."

"How is that possible?"

"Let's find out. I'd like you to ask some questions silently within yourself—and tell me whatever comes into your mind in response."

She looked skeptical but nodded in agreement.

"Good. So ask inside: Would this part be willing to communicate with us in consciousness?"

She closed her eyes; then opened them wide. "Yes, it will talk to us. But it sounds really mean."

"Does it have something specific that it wants to say?"

"No. Just that you're wasting your time."

"How so?" I asked.

"It says this isn't going to work."

"Okay. Well, thank the part for its comment, and ask if it will continue talking to us anyway."

Pearl shrugged. "Why not?"

"I'd like you to ask the part how it feels about this person called Pearl."

"It says it doesn't like me. I'm a complete screw-up."

"Can it be more specific?"

"I can't do anything right. I'm fat. Nobody likes me. I have no friends."

"Interesting. Anything else?"

"I give too much; then get upset when people are mean."

"Go on."

"I can't stand up for myself."

She was looking at me wide-eyed as she delivered this cruel

assessment of herself.

"Ask the monster if it enjoys what it's doing to you," I prompted.

"It says I'm stupid so I'm never going to amount to anything anyway. I mess up everything I do. It says it has to watch over me all the time."

I wanted to offer Pearl some reassurance, to let her know that these private thoughts, which were now coming out and being heard by a stranger, were strictly one-sided and would not affect my opinion of her.

"These are very cutting words," I said. "I certainly don't agree with them, but it's important that we give the part a chance to express itself without being fought off."

She nodded, though her tension was palpable.

"Isn't it interesting that it says it has to watch over you," I commented.

"Yes, it seems to think it's my guardian angel." She gave an incredulous laugh.

"Well, ask this monster-guardian what it's trying to accomplish with these harsh judgments."

Closing her eyes, she sat in silence for a moment. "It says it wants to protect me," she said finally. "Can that be true?"

"It could indeed be true," I assured her.

She looked at me speculatively, considering this novel idea. "You know, I think it really does want to protect me. But I sure don't like how it's doing it."

"Did you hear what Pearl had to say to you?" I asked the part.

"I do it for her own good," it snapped back.

"Can you tell us what you are protecting her from?"

Pearl gave me a rueful look. "From making a total fool of herself."

Knowing that in their original state our parts are not pitted against us in this way, I wondered what circumstances or events had started this one on its present relentless course.

"When did you first decide that Pearl needed protection?" I asked it.

Pearl gazed at her hands and when she looked up her eyes were filled with tears.

"It was after my brother died."

Speaking through sobs, she explained that she had been twelve when her brother Kenny had died of leukemia. He'd been bedridden for a long time but nobody had told her the nature of his illness — or that he might not survive. One evening, as she was leaving for swimming practice, she yelled goodbye to him from the bottom of the stairs. When she came home later that night, he was dead.

"I didn't even say a proper goodbye."

Kenny had been her only friend, she told me. Without him, she felt completely alone.

"It must have been a few weeks afterwards that I overheard my parents talking. It was late and I was supposed to be in bed. They'd been drinking as usual and got into an argument, with each blaming the other for Kenny's illness. Then I heard Dad say: 'If only it had been Pearl who died.'"

I held her hand as she recalled this hurtful scene. Her anguish seemed as fresh and vivid as it must have been at the time — nearly twenty years before.

After Kenny's death her mother's problems intensified. She had always been dependent on alcohol and pills, but now she was in and out of the mental ward of the local hospital for her depression. It wasn't long before she was permanently institutionalized.

"I visited her every week all through my teens. I guess I was looking for some sort of comfort, but whenever I complained about anything she always said the same thing: 'Wait till you're an adult — it gets worse.'"

Things didn't improve when Pearl and her father were the only ones left at home.

"He picked on everything I did. It was a matter of policy, he told me—to keep me from getting a swelled head."

She knew it was impossible to please him but kept on trying anyway.

"I had to prove I was worthy since I was a girl and I wasn't my brother."

As Pearl related these bitter memories I noticed that she had become quite childlike in her manner. The tears and sobbing, combined with her air of bewilderment and helplessness, told me that we were no longer talking to the monster—or guardian as it had now become. This was a new and different part of Pearl, a part still overwhelmed by feelings that were nearly two decades old. When I asked this new part how old it was, it promptly replied that it was twelve.

Ideally, our parts develop along with us, but we all have at least a few that have failed to grow up and go on viewing the world from a child's perspective. Different parts have different reasons for staying behind. Pearl's twelve-year-old had gotten bogged down in traumatic events, unable to extricate herself from painful and confused feelings. On top of that, she had developed what some psychologists might call a Peter Pan complex, a determined resistance to growing up. Not only had the part heard the mother's warning that life gets worse when you're an adult, she had seen the evidence: The mother herself had become progressively more bitter and unstable as she aged, finally entering a mental institution—a striking example of her own dismal prophecy.

I thanked the twelve-year-old part for coming forward and asked her to observe while we continued talking to the guardian. As we soon discovered, it too had been infected by the mother's warning—firmly believing that Pearl would be miserable if she tried to compete in an adult world. I decided to avoid tangling with the guardian on this issue and asked it instead: "How do you see grown-ups in general?"

"They're miserable," it replied.

"How old do you think Pearl is?"

"It thinks I'm twelve," Pearl answered.

The part's strategy for "protecting" Pearl was to keep her in a holding pattern. Its ridicule was meant to prevent her from trying new things or taking on challenges that could lead her away from the safe haven of childhood.

"You've really excelled at your work," I told the guardian, quite sincerely. "As Pearl has confirmed, you've done an excellent job of holding her back in life. How did you learn to criticize so effectively?"

Warming to the praise, the part candidly revealed that it had used Pearl's father as a role model, though it had learned a few things about carping and nagging from the mother as well. As it boasted about these achievements Pearl began to see how closely its agenda resembled that of her parents. This was an eye-opener for her, as it is for most of us when we realize to what extent we have internalized our parents' views of us, however hurtful.

But in spite of these revelations, the guardian part did not seem to recognize the damage it was doing.

"Did you hear Pearl call you a monster?" I gently chided. "Can you see how tormented and depressed you've been making her feel?"

Pearl flushed, presumably on the part's behalf. "He says that he didn't know any other way."

I noticed that she had referred to the part as "he" for the first time—perhaps an indication that she was beginning to empathize with this errant aspect of herself.

"Of course he didn't," I agreed. "But ask him to think about it. He says he wants to protect you from the misery of growing up, and yet you already feel miserable now."

"That's true."

"So which is worse?" I asked the guardian. "The misery caused by your constant criticism or the risk of letting her grow up? And what would happen if she did grow up and found out that she had talents and abilities far beyond what her parents allowed?"

Pearl blinked several times. "He wants to know if you think that's likely."

"Well," I mused, "if it is likely, wouldn't it be important to find out?"

She nodded thoughtfully.

"Ask the part: Would he like to discover a better way of protecting Pearl?"

"Yes, I think he would."

"Tell him thank you — we appreciate that. And ask him to consider what he's been telling us. He learned everything he knows from Mom and Dad — can he remember ever being without that influence?"

She shook her head.

"Would he like to find out how that would be?"

"What would he have to do?" She narrowed her eyes.

"Well, let's ask him to look at what he took from your parents: the ridicule, fault-finding, warnings about growing up, all those criticisms that did not originate within him and are not his own. Can he push all that over to one side?"

Not surprisingly, the part responded with wariness. As he intuitively knew, his whole identity was wrapped up in his parental role-playing. What would be left if he gave that up?

I assured him that by giving up what did not belong to him, he would not cease to exist. On the contrary, it would be a way to touch base with himself, to discover his place within Pearl's own identity. Finally, when I said that it needn't be more than an experiment, he agreed to try.

"Ask him to look inside himself," I instructed. "Can he tell the difference between his own energy and the energies he took from others?"

"Yes, there is a difference."

"What does he notice?"

"He hears their voices."

The part could discern within himself the sarcastic tones of Pearl's father. Mom's warnings were there too, along with some murky energy that the part identified as the bitterness and disappointment of both parents.

"Can he push those things over to one side?"

Pearl nodded, seeming deep in concentration.

I waited a moment and then asked: "How is he feeling now?"

"Relieved. We both feel relieved."

"Is he happy with the experiment?"

"Yes. He doesn't want that stuff anymore. He wants to know what to do with it."

I instructed the part to create a large (imaginary) container in the room where we were sitting and to begin moving the parents' energy out of himself and into the container. This is a process that I call a psychic-emotive release. It is an act of consciously imagining emotional overlays to be released, and gives a powerful message to the subconscious. Above all, it symbolizes a commitment to placing one's own truth over and above the negative examples and teachings of others.

Such a release usually leaves a part feeling disoriented and this was the case with Pearl's guardian. I suggested to Pearl that she connect with the part by reaching out to him with her mind and heart, welcoming him home. She closed her eyes and a minute or two ticked by.

"How did he respond?" I prompted.

Her voice was strained. "I think he wanted to respond but now he's turned his back on me."

"What does that mean?"

"He doesn't want anything to do with me."

"Does he know that he's a part of you?"

"He doesn't believe that."

"Hmm. Well, let him know that you are the same Pearl as the twelve-year-old, only you've grown up. Tell him that nearly twenty years have passed and that you have survived to become a biological adult."

"He says none of that can be true."

"Why not try showing him a picture of yourself, just as you are today—thirty years old, attractive, independent. And show him some scenes from your life: your home, your roommates, your work as a lifeguard. This will all be very surprising to him—so be sure to give him some reassurance."

After a moment Pearl sighed and shook her head. "He says we're lying."

All attempts to create a bond between Pearl and the guardian proved futile. The part simply refused to believe that he had any connection to this grown-up stranger claiming to be Pearl. The Pearl that he knew was a child of twelve—helpless, incompetent and dependent on his guidance.

The guardian's devotion to the twelve-year-old was touching but it was creating problems. I had hoped that the bonding would be straightforward, allowing the part to move easily to the next stage of the process—the rollover. He had done a good psychic-emotive release and this is usually a turning point. But the part remained sullen and uncooperative.

The fact that Pearl felt little affection for the guardian didn't help. She admitted that she was uncomfortable trying to bond with a part that had spent so many years putting her down. Now that we had hit this patch of resistance the session was dragging— and to make matters worse Pearl began to distract from the problem at hand by raising concerns about money. I was charging her by the hour and she was fretting about how long the session was taking. She even insisted that we take a break to calculate how much money she had spent so far.

I calmed her as best I could and explained that the part's resistance was natural. His job, after all, had always been to protect the twelve-year-old and he had already told us that he didn't trust adults. Why should he accept Pearl as authentic or believe her far-fetched tales?

"I have an idea," I said finally. "Let's back off and give him some space while we talk to the twelve-year-old. He cares about her—so maybe helping her will help him."

In welcome contrast, this child part lived inside the body and already knew that she belonged to Pearl. Not only had she been listening to our conversation, she had longed to reach out to Pearl when the guardian had turned his back. All the same, she was dismayed to learn that Pearl had arrived at the advanced age of thirty.

Pearl and her parts had expressed so much reluctance around the idea of growing up that I thought it was time for a discussion on the subject. I began by suggesting that growing up might not be all bad.

"When you grow up your life isn't run by adults, you get to make your own decisions and you have way more freedom to be who you are."

"But grown-ups don't have any fun," Pearl objected.

I asked her to recall how parents interacted with their children at the swimming pool where she worked as a lifeguard.

"Do all the adults look miserable?"

"Well, no," she reflected. "Actually, most of them seem to be having fun."

"Ask the twelve-year-old if she can see that."

"Yes."

"And tell me, Pearl, what do you think allows those adults to be happy?"

She twisted a strand of hair in her fingers. "Well, they couldn't have had parents like mine."

"You're probably right," I conceded. "Can you imagine what kind of a grown-up you would be if your parents had been more positive?"

"I would be completely different," she said.

I asked the twelve-year-old if she'd ever dreamed about that difference and how it would be. The future had always appeared dull, she said. She used to think about growing up and becoming a nurse so she could take care of Kenny, yet in this vision of the future Kenny himself had always remained a child.

I pondered how deep and fundamental the link was between the twelve-year-old and the guardian. The two parts were like two sides of a coin, with similar values and complementary agendas. Both carried feelings of loss and rejection, but while the guardian believed that you get hurt if you care about people, the twelve-year-old was a pleaser and would do anything for acceptance. The two parts also shared feelings of unworthiness, expressed by the guardian as "you're no good" and by the twelve-year-old as "I'm no good." The main difference between them was that the twelve-year-old had imitated the mother while the guardian had taken more from the father.

Having watched the guardian release his parental overlay, the twelve-year-old was eager to follow suit. Her main contribution to the trash container was the addiction-and-depression pattern inherited from her mother—this was what had really been weighing her down. When I asked her to form a picture of this mental-illness pattern she envisioned an intricate crystalline structure, beautiful, fragile and oppressive. Taking great care, she was able to pick the whole thing up in one piece and drop it into the bin. Hitting bottom, it shattered into a million tiny shards, each one razor sharp.

We knew that the twelve-year-old had been miserable at the

time of her brother's death, but it was my guess that it hadn't started there. My hunch was proved right when I asked her to look back through her own memory. She recalled a long string of hurts and injustices, all of them perpetrated by Mom and Dad. These parents were truly toxic. They forced her to go to school when she was sick, slapped her for taking initiative and bullied her if she cried. With each remembered incident came a fresh sense of outrage, and the incidents seemed endless. I began to wonder if we would ever find a clearing in the thicket of sorrows when, most unexpectedly, we came upon a little patch of contentment.

"I'm a small baby," she said, a soft light coming into her eyes. "I'm lying on a blanket in the grass. The sun is shining." She smiled and tilted her head back, as if to recapture the sun's warmth on her face.

"Is there anyone with you?"

"Granny is working in her garden. She's tending her roses." She gestured to one side and then lapsed into a reverie. "Granny's roses covered the entire back wall of her house and grew all along the fence. Their perfume filled the whole neighborhood. I can smell it even now."

"Ask the baby, basking in the sun on her blanket: How does she feel about Granny?"

"She loves Granny."

"And does Granny love the baby?"

"Granny adores the baby."

"Is this a surprise?"

She shrugged. "It's just the way things are."

I had to smile. We had just spent the good part of an hour in the valley of endless betrayal, yet now the part was confident that loving and being loved were life's most natural gifts.

"So the baby feels loved, and she accepts that as natural. How does she feel about life in general?"

"She finds it exciting," said Pearl. "She feels really warm and happy inside."

I was pleased to see that the worried, somewhat pinched look had left Pearl's face, replaced by a happy glow. We had finally drifted into a layer of memory in which the part felt at peace with herself and the world. I was tempted to look for an even deeper connection to self, but knew that if I took the part further back in time—to the womb, for instance—it would once again be bombarded by the mother's depression. This would dishearten Pearl and extend the length of the session, quite possibly rekindling her money concerns. I could see that the good feelings the part had uncovered were vivid and real to her, and would provide a strong enough base on which to build. Somewhat reluctantly, therefore, I decided to work with what we had—this bright little tableau in an otherwise bleak landscape.

"Ask the baby—as she's enjoying the warm, happy energy of the garden—to look forward through her life. How would things have been different if she had held onto this excitement at being alive, this knowledge of loving and being loved?"

Pearl took a moment to reflect.

"I wouldn't have been so desperate for my parents' approval. They were unhappy and needed someone to blame—but it wasn't my fault."

One of my strongest convictions is that life offers us infinite chances to change our minds. It is never too late to revisit times and places where we lost touch with ourselves and to reconsider the choices we made there. I asked Pearl's part to look again at some of the turning points in her life, points where she made such pivotal decisions as: *I have to prove I'm worthy … grown-ups don't have any fun … the future is dull … I'm no good.*

"What do you think now of those beliefs?" I asked.

"I know I'm a good person. I don't need to prove my worth."

There are always positive beliefs inherent within a rollover, though they may not be coded in language. These beliefs are basic assumptions—things that are self-evident to the part—but without language they tend to get lost or forgotten and so I usually spend time helping a part to identify and formalize them. Pearl's part, basking in the sunny garden and the glow of Granny's love, came up with the core beliefs: *life is exciting ... loving and being loved are natural ... I'm a good person ... I love myself.*

There was just one step left to take. I asked the part to expand the love and warmth it felt in the garden and begin bringing that energy forward through time, dissolving the old beliefs and replacing them with the new. When the part had come all the way to the present, Pearl opened her eyes and smiled.

"She's happy to be here."

"Does she still feel like a twelve-year-old?"

"More like eighteen."

"Would she like to continue growing up?"

"Yes."

I suggested to the part that she grow up over the coming weeks. She happily agreed, already looking forward to joining Pearl in the adult world.

With the twelve-year-old thus removed from his care the guardian was shaken, but he was now willing to face reality. When I asked him to search his own past to see if he too could find the sunny rose garden, it took him only a moment to recall the scene—Granny was there working amongst her flowers and the baby was musing happily. There was just one problem: He couldn't locate himself in the memory. He knew he had been there because the picture was vivid in every detail—but where was he?

"Let's think about it," I said. "When we first began working today, Pearl located you just behind her left shoulder—so we know that you've been habituated to living outside the body. But chances are you were not always outside. Why not try looking inside baby Pearl?"

Although alarmed by the prospect he did take a look and he

did find himself inside the baby. After taking some time to get used to it, he decided that it wasn't so bad after all. In fact, he was finding it warm and cozy inside.

"What are his feelings about baby Pearl?"

"He likes her."

"Does he still think she's a loser?"

"No, he finds her very bright. He knows she'll do well at whatever she tries."

I asked the guardian what job he did for Pearl back then when she was an infant.

"I observe what's going on around her and keep her out of harm's way."

"Ah," I said, delighted. "He's an observer part. Ask him: How was he communicating with Pearl at that time, before he learned about criticism from Mom and Dad?"

"He was just there. He supported me."

Observer parts are very common and seem to belong to our innate survival equipment. Most often they watch without interfering but sometimes they do step in. Oftentimes they're highly clairvoyant, anticipating danger in advance and steering us to safety. Pearl later came to the conclusion that it was her guardian who had turned her around the evening of my lecture, somehow foreseeing that our meeting would prove worthwhile.

Having located himself in the rose garden, the guardian was able to follow the twelve-year-old's path to the present. But there was a problem. When he had come all the way through to now, I found to my dismay that he was no longer inside Pearl's body, but had resumed his old post just behind her left shoulder. Although he had been integrated with baby Pearl at the rollover, force of habit had caused him to separate as he came through time.

I have since learned to circumvent this problem—either by resolving the issues around the dissociation or by using specific verbal guidance as the part brings the rollover forward. I hadn't done this with the guardian, however, and so was left having to coax him back into the body — a very trying task as it turned out. Clearly recalling Pearl's habitual state of anguish, the part told us flatly that being in the body was too painful — he would rather stay where he was.

I asked Pearl for her views on the matter. Would she like the part to come into her body? She too was reluctant. I knew she had not fully realized how much the part had changed. To her, this was more or less the same old monster as before — any minute now the verbal abuse would begin. It was bad enough coming from a part that hovered outside her body. Why on earth would she want to bring him in?

I reminded her that the part had not been a monster when she was a baby. On the contrary, he had been full of confidence in her strength and abilities.

To the guardian, I said, "Why not give it a try? Now that we've cleared out Mom's depression and Dad's ridicule, and Pearl is feeling good about herself, it may be pleasant to go in."

The part remained hesitant, and so I suggested that he send a tiny feeler into Pearl's body.

"If you don't like it you can bring it right back out."

This seemed safe enough and he agreed to try. He cautiously sent in first one feeler and then another, and pretty soon he got his foot in, so to speak. Bit by bit he eased himself in, stopping to reconnoiter at every stage along the way. I must say, the part really took his time getting back into the body, but in the end our patience was rewarded. When he was finally in he suddenly began having *déja vu*. Vividly recalling all the nuances of thought and feeling he had shared with Pearl as a baby, he decided that he really did belong inside her, that this was his true home and that he could now resume his original job of watching over her and giving her "good intuition."

The session thus came to an end. It seemed it had taken us three days to do this work, but in fact it was only eight hours. As I accompanied Pearl to the door I asked her to give me a call when she felt ready for another session. Although we had made good progress there was no way of knowing what effect our efforts would have on the bulimia. We had chosen to work with the guardian because he was causing Pearl so much immediate distress — but at no point had we asked him what he contributed to the eating disorder, if anything. Meanwhile, we hadn't even touched on the issue of food.

Pearl was back for a second session just two weeks later. I didn't get any feedback from her when she called for her appointment, and so was still in the dark as to what her progress had been. As I showed her in and took her jacket she purposely tormented me by putting on a glum face — her idea of a joke. When we finally got settled she gave me a radiant smile.

"You won't believe it," she said.

There had been just three bulimic episodes since our session — a striking improvement on her usual regime, which involved multiple episodes on a daily basis. It had been years, she said, since she'd abstained for more than a day. Now, on most days, she was eating normal meals and keeping them down. She had even put on a little weight.

Our spontaneous celebration took the form of hooting, hugging and singing. When we finally calmed down and resumed our seats my thoughts turned to the three recent bulimic bouts.

"Pearl, I'd like you to think back. Can you remember the events leading up to those episodes? Do you know what set them off?"

She had already given this some thought, and said that they had followed closely on occasions when she felt criticized or rejected. It seemed to her that these were the feelings that had always brought on her bulimic episodes, right from the start.

"It was no wonder I had so many, with the monster always on my case."

"And now that the monster is an observer and is supporting you, it makes sense that you feel more secure and less inclined to binge."

"Yes, but there's still the criticism that comes from the outside, from other people."

When I asked her to describe the symptoms of an approaching episode, she said it was like "needing a fix." There was an overwhelming sense of urgency: Her heart rate increased, her ears rang and she felt light-headed. The dark void that was always gnawing away at her became voracious and insatiable. The only thing that could appease her was food, and once she began eating she couldn't stop because it was so pleasurable. Even as she spoke, red blotches appeared on her cheeks and her eyes took on a glassy look.

"Is there something this eating part would like to tell us?"

"It's dying to talk to us."

The part wanted to say how upset it had been with the changes in Pearl. "It was me who kept you awake at night," it announced.

"So that's what was going on," Pearl exclaimed, throwing her hands up dramatically.

Normally a sound sleeper, she had spent several nights tossing and turning, though she'd forgotten to tell me this.

The part claimed full responsibility for the eating binges. Its one and only purpose in life, it said, was to bring Pearl pleasure, and it believed that getting her to eat was the fastest, easiest way to do that—and the safest.

"I give her pleasure with very few consequences."

Eating was a private indulgence, hidden from other people and their judgments, and it didn't involve drugs or alcohol, which had ruined her mother's life. It made up for a bad day, eased the pain of rejection and soothed feelings of inadequacy.

This seemed a straightforward enough agenda but it made me pause. I asked the eating part what it knew about the other side of the bulimia — the throwing up.

"It's not responsible for that," Pearl said.

"So who has been doing the throwing up?" I asked.

With a little backtracking we were able to pin the badge on the twelve-year-old (now eighteen, going on thirty). I was intrigued, since in my other cases involving bulimics I had found one part doing both jobs. A duo of this kind was unique in my experience — and all the more anomalous because each part was acting independently — barely aware of the other's existence. While the eater was busy bringing Pearl pleasure and comfort through food, the twelve-year-old was committed to throwing up to keep her slim and attractive (essential to the part's youthful self-image as well as her need to please).

During our previous session this picture had shifted. With the twelve-year-old growing up and getting love and support from within, the old feelings of rejection, which had long been the eater's cue to go into action, were hardly present at all. This had thrown the eater into a tail spin, since there was now very little call for its services. I could just see the part lying in wait for Pearl to feel a twinge of the old inadequacy, and then pouncing on the opportunity to get a good food binge going. It had so far succeeded on three separate occasions.

I have consistently found parts to be completely committed to the work they do. When the inner ecology begins to shift, as Pearl's was doing, any part that finds itself dislodged will make an effort to continue doing its job. Parts don't usually have the ability to think for themselves or make adjustments in their own behavior. The subconscious consists mainly of programmed energy, and needs information and guidance from the conscious mind in order to make changes. In fact, parts actually look to the conscious mind for instruction. And so Pearl's eater was unable to change its ways, and if left unchecked it might have eventually succeeded in drawing Pearl back into the old pattern.

"Are you aware that Pearl doesn't like what you've been doing?" I asked the eater.

"The part doesn't really understand that."

"Well then, let's clarify it. Pearl, what do you consciously see as the consequences of the bulimic pattern?"

Giving it some thought, she came up with a list: it made her antisocial, caused her personal humiliation and kept her from focusing on anything worthwhile—like getting a better job or going back to school.

"Did the part hear that? How does it respond?"

"It says it's sorry. It didn't know."

"Tell it we do appreciate its good intentions. And ask it: Would it like to find a new way of bringing Pearl pleasure?—a way that is free of all these consequences that she mentioned?"

"Yes."

"Good—tell it thank you. And ask the part to look back through its store of memories. What are some of the ways it brought Pearl pleasure in the past, before it started binge eating?"

Pearl sank into her chair, gazing into the near distance. Her face softened as she recalled an abundance of childhood joys, fondly describing such pleasures as cycling, playing checkers, learning to knit and watching the light fade at dusk.

"Do some of these things still bring Pearl pleasure?"

"It's not the same."

"How is it not the same?"

"Pearl was happy then. It was easy to give her pleasure."

"Does this part know when she stopped being happy?"

"When Kenny died."

"Ask the part: What did you decide to do about it?"

"Look for better ways to give her pleasure."

"Interesting. Can the part tell us more about this?"

The eater recalled several years of heavy partying, starting when Pearl was eighteen. The sex and drugs had felt good for a while, but Pearl had tried too hard to please the men she met and ended up feeling used and rejected. When she finally swore off men altogether the part was at a loss as to how it could bring pleasure into her life. That's when her depression had set in. Some time later, it hit on the idea of binge eating.

"So stronger forms of pleasure were necessary as Pearl became more unhappy," I remarked.

"Yes, I guess that's true. Pleasure became a substitute for happiness."

"Ask the part: What do you think would happen if Pearl's new-found happiness turned out to be permanent?"

Pearl chewed on her lip. "I guess I wouldn't need a substitute then."

As the eater continued moving back through time, it revealed itself to be a true hedonist, remembering the good times and forgetting all the rest. As an eight-year-old the part was caught up in the magic of fairy tales and storybook characters; at five and six it reveled in Santa Claus and Easter Bunny. As it continued to explore, it came across one pleasure-filled memory after another, and so when it did stumble on a hard spot I sat up and took notice.

"I see a small baby lying alone under bright lights," said Pearl.

"What is the baby feeling," I asked with concern, noticing that she was hugging herself and looking pale.

"Cold and alone," she said. Her voice had gone small and faint.

"Ask the baby if Mother is there."

"No, Mother isn't here."

"Is anyone with her?"

"There are other babies in the room."

"Can she tell us where she is?"

"It's a hospital."

Knowing that in many hospitals babies are removed from their mothers' care soon after birth, I guessed that this was the problem here—Pearl had likely been taken straight from the womb to a brightly lit room where the nursing staff could keep an eye on her. Whether or not my guess was correct, the experience was clearly a traumatic one.

I suggested to Pearl that she intervene by putting her adult self in the picture.

"Let her know that you are her future self. She may be a little startled at first."

"She's happy to see me."

"Will she let you pick her up?"

"She wants me to."

As Pearl reached out to her tiny former self, taking her gently in her arms, I was relieved to see some of the color return to her face. But the pair had barely enough time to get acquainted before Pearl was swept back to an even earlier memory. This time, she told me, the setting was the delivery room shortly after her birth.

I confess to inwardly bracing myself. Over the years I've worked with countless parts that have remembered birth, and nearly all of them have been traumatized by their experience of entering the world. You can imagine my surprise then, when Pearl gave me a bright look and said that her part was happy to be born. Getting out of the womb and starting to live life was this part's idea of a genuine thrill.

"Are you still there with the baby? Does she know who you are?"

"Yes, I've taken her from one of the nurses — I almost had to yank to get her away." She laughed gleefully. "I've told them that I'm her, thirty years later, and that I've come back for her."

I could picture the infant cradled in Pearl's arms, and there was no mistaking the infectious warmth that radiated from the two of them. I reminded myself that this baby was the same eater we had been talking to all along — she was now simply at an earlier stage of development. It was clear that this part of Pearl had been involved with pleasure right from the start, so zestful was she about being alive. Here, at her base, she took pleasure in everything, but now her pleasure equaled real happiness—happiness without compromise and with no substitutions needed. When I asked her if she could put this feeling into words, she said, "I enjoy living each moment for the moment, because every moment is magical."

No longer something squeezed into fictions and fairy tales, magic was now all-pervasive for the part, an essential aspect of life itself. All that remained was to integrate this talent for happiness with Pearl's life in the present. The part found it easy to surge its energy forward through the events of Pearl's life. As it did so, Pearl radiated pleasure. Afterwards, she reported that a whole pathway of her mind had melted away and reformed itself.

We both had very positive feelings as the session came to an end. I was aware, of course, that bulimia is considered extremely difficult to treat, and that many people would not believe an expedient cure possible. Yet it seemed to me that what we had accomplished might be enough.

Before Pearl left I made a point of giving her some practical guidelines for eating. If her bulimia was indeed over and done with she would now be in a position to put some new habits in place. My main suggestion was that she listen to her body and respond to its needs, eating when she was hungry, stopping when she was full and eating as often or as seldom as she felt the need.

"Don't eat when you're not hungry, even if it's meal time, and never eat just because people put pressure on you."

Just two weeks later she called with exciting news. There had been no bulimic episodes—none at all. She had not overeaten and she had not thrown up. She hadn't even felt the urge. Nor was there any sign of anorexia.

Today, more than ten years later, Pearl's eating disorder has not returned. In a recent letter she wrote, "No matter how stressful life gets, it never occurs to me to go back to being bulimic." Meanwhile, free of the demands made by the bulimia on her time and concentration, and with her parts helping to enhance her self-esteem, she was finally able to fulfill her dream of putting herself through university. Before our work, she told me, she had never considered herself to be "university material." I felt pleased and proud when she graduated with top marks.

———————

My work with Pearl reminded me above all that the labels "anorexic" and "bulimic" describe little more than superficial behavior patterns. When you probe beneath the surface of an eating disorder there are many surprises in store. I have yet to find an internal environment or belief system that is the same in any two cases.

That said, I can add that certain patterns do recur, for example, the feeling of not being good enough and the sense of an interior void or black hole. Voids are by no means exclusive to bulimics. Many people have that gnawing sense of emptiness at their core, but different people cope with it in different ways. A void often begins with a childhood experience of abandonment—a sense of being left in total isolation, without input or answers, as had happened to Pearl when her brother died. When a part actually leaves the body, as her guardian part did, this confirms and deepens the feeling of emptiness.

Working with the guardian I saw once again that dissociated parts get badly out of touch with the feelings, perceptions and daily reality of the person they belong to—and because they are out of touch they can be highly resistant to the updating process. The guardian accused us of lying when we showed him scenes from Pearl's adult life. Taking a direct approach to persuade such a part to integrate is rarely successful. Working with the issues around the dissociation and with related parts is usually what makes the transition possible. The guardian was able to make the necessary adjustments only after the twelve-year-old it had been guarding so diligently began to grow up.

I found it interesting that Pearl's three parts—the twelve-year-old, the monster/guardian and the eater—made up a perfect Karpman triangle, that is, an interlinked family of victim, persecutor and rescuer. This archetypal pattern, named after the psychologist who identified it, tends to reflect the structure of myth and fairy tales. In Pearl's case we had an innocent heroine bullied by an evil monster, with a pleasure-seeking fairy godmother to the rescue—a good illustration of how we create identity at subconscious levels. Yet, even in our adaptation of archetypes, we are endlessly inventive, as the cases in this book attest.

I Deserve to Die

June of 1985 was still early days for me as a therapist. I had put together my basic approach just a year before, and although I'd spent countless hours working with a range of psychological problems, my experience with physical illness was limited. All the same, I had accumulated some successes in working with complaints like allergies, asthma, insomnia, headaches and a variety of minor physical stresses, and was eager to continue exploring the possibilities.

Alex had undergone surgery for colon cancer, and while that seemed to be under control, recent tests had revealed that his liver was now afflicted. His doctors had pronounced this new malignancy untreatable and given him a year to live. Having heard through the grapevine that I was offering free research sessions to people with physical complaints, he called for an appointment and described his condition over the phone. I admit I was intrigued by the prospect of working with a disease that was thought to be incurable. I agreed to see him but told him quite pointedly that I had no experience with such serious illness and might not be able to help him. All the same, I suspect that his imagination embellished what he had heard about me and that, when he arrived at my door, he was privately hoping for a one-shot miracle cure.

At the time, I was still working out of my tiny apartment in downtown Vancouver, where two comfortable chairs in the living room provided the setting for my sessions. As I ushered Alex in and invited him to sit down, I thought that I had never met anyone so shy and nervous. I did my best to put him at ease with a chatty commentary on the weather but his eyes continued to dart about the room and he said very little.

Still a young man, Alex was a bit on the stocky side and not very tall. I noticed immediately how well groomed he was—his cotton pants and shirt were immaculately pressed, and everything about him was exceptionally neat and tidy. He had fine blond hair and blue eyes, and these, augmented by his tendency to blush, gave him an attractive boyish look. All in all, he struck me as a gentle, mild-mannered soul. He certainly betrayed no hint of the rigid fundamentalist beliefs and strange "secret" that were soon to emerge.

I started the session by gathering preliminary information. He told me that he was thirty-six and that his trade was repairing clocks and watches, but that he hadn't worked since his cancer was diagnosed. A bachelor, he lived alone in a highrise apartment building, where he now spent his time sleeping and watching TV. When I asked him about family he said that he was an only child and had little contact with his parents, who lived in another city. He lacked a social life except for a few nodding acquaintances at the church he attended. As our conversation progressed I got the impression that he felt completely alone in the world and saw himself as a really unlucky guy.

Conversing with Alex wasn't easy. Each time I asked him a question he blushed, answered in a few words, and then fell silent. Avoiding my gaze, he fidgeted endlessly with a signet ring that he wore on the ring finger of his right hand—first turning it round and round and then sliding it back and forth. Normally at ease in the company of other people, I was finding his nervousness infectious and decided to start in on a process with no further preamble.

"We could approach this in a number of ways," I began, "but

I'm wondering if there's a part of you that will answer directly for your illness. So let's try for that and see what happens."

He gave me a blank look.

"Let me explain. I'll ask you a question and I'd like you to direct the question inward and wait for a response. It's important to accept whatever answer you get, whether it comes in words, images, thoughts, feelings or whatever. Would you like to try it?"

He nodded.

"What I'd like you to do, then, is focus inside and ask if the part of you that's in charge of your illness — that's responsible for creating it in the first place and that has kept it going ever since — ask that part if it would be willing to communicate."

Alex stopped fidgeting and seemed to concentrate. After a minute or two he looked up and said, "No, not really."

"Did you get any reply at all?"

"No."

This was a fairly typical beginning. Many people tend to discount their initial responses, and I could see from Alex's frown and the tilt of his head that he wasn't really drawing a blank.

"I wonder if you could tell me what just came into your mind," I coaxed. "It might not seem relevant right now but things don't always make sense right away, so it's important to report whatever we get."

He again began twisting his ring and admitted that he had recalled a scene from his childhood, at the same time protesting that it couldn't possibly have anything to do with his illness. With further encouragement, however, he at last began to describe the memory.

Between the ages of seven and ten, he said, he had lived with his parents in a small village in Haiti, where his father worked as a Christian missionary. He recalled standing outside his house watching the local children playing in the street. He couldn't join in because he was forbidden to have any contact with the villagers, who—according to his father—were "heathens."

Alex related this memory in a halting manner—it was a period of his life that he hadn't thought about for a long time. But as he continued his face began to color and a hint of resentment crept into his voice.

"My father was strict—you couldn't go against him. If you did, well, he had this leather strap that he used."

I got him to ask his part why it had shown him this memory.

"The part says it has a secret."

Intrigued, I suggested that he ask the part what would happen if it told us its secret. At this Alex hesitated. "The part says that I would get in trouble and might even die."

He himself had no inkling what secret the part was referring to, though his childhood in Haiti was coming back to him with surprising vividness. Along with the other white children in the village, he said, he attended a school run by the wives of the missionaries. He remembered feeling bored in class. Strange, he remarked, but even as he recalled this he could feel the old restlessness coming over him.

"I took no interest in my lessons. I used to wish that I could be one of the village boys—they had more freedom and more fun."

In spite of the prohibition he did sometimes sneak off with the local children, even visiting with their families. He recalled being mesmerized by the frightening stories the villagers told, which centered around sorcery and sacrificial rites. The religion they practiced was voodoo, he explained, giving me a shy grin.

Having become animated while reporting these details, Alex again retreated into skepticism. He didn't see the point of dredging up this ancient history, he told me in a flat voice. How could it possibly have anything to do with his cancer? I replied that he might be right, but since this was the response he had received when he asked for the part in charge of the cancer, I thought we should pay attention, at least till we found out where it was leading.

"We don't know yet why the part might be showing you these memories but we did ask it to speak with us. I think we should at least give it a chance to communicate."

I had noticed in particular how eager the part was to tell us it had a secret. My feeling was that it wanted to let us in on it as a way of unburdening itself.

"Why not ask the part if it would be willing to share its secret with us," I suggested.

I waited as Alex communed with his part, fully expecting his resistance to block our progress. But a moment later his eyes popped open and his face turned bright red.

"The tree!" he sputtered. "I'd forgotten about the tree."

Gripping the arms of his chair he stared glassy-eyed at the space in front of him, uttering a succession of short, nonsensical phrases. Whatever memory the part had brought to his mind was obviously a very alarming one. I urged him to stay conscious and try to simply observe what his part was showing him, but he appeared oblivious to my words and even my presence. I knew that I would not get a coherent story out of him till both he and his part calmed down.

Taking firm hold of his hands, I spoke to him in a tone that was commanding yet gentle. "Alex, look at me. I'm right here. Alex, come back."

After several minutes of this his eyes began to focus, and as he gradually came round he sat blinking in evident confusion. I took some time to soothe and reassure him. Then I began to go over the sequence of events that had brought us to this point, partly to clarify matters for myself but also to get his conscious mind more grounded in the present.

"We asked to speak to the part of you that's in charge of your illness and the part responded by showing you some memories from your childhood in Haiti—a time that you had almost forgotten. We weren't sure if these memories could have anything to do with your illness but decided that they were worth investigating. Then the part told us it had a secret and this prompted more memories, for instance, the fact that you were bored at school and that you had some contact with the village boys. When we asked the part to tell us its secret, that's when you remembered something about a tree.

"Are you with me on this?" I asked, noticing him drifting away again.

With some effort he managed to refocus his attention.

"Is the part still with you?"

"Yes."

I asked him what had caused his alarm but he still couldn't talk about it without extreme agitation. I thought I knew what the problem might be and decided to change direction.

"I want you to ask this part how old it thinks you are."

He looked confused.

"Ask the part this question: How old do you think Alex is?"

Alex asked and the part promptly replied that he was nine. On further questioning, it revealed not the slightest doubt that he still lived with his parents in Haiti. Unaware of the years that had passed, the part was stuck in a time warp, utterly consumed by the feelings and concerns that had occupied Alex as a boy.

I'm not sure how much of this Alex himself understood. As he reported the part's answers he kept getting that faraway look that told me he had lost contact with the present. It seemed that he'd become so identified with the part and with whatever alarming memory it was showing him that he couldn't remember who he was or where he was.

"We'd better let the part know how many years have passed and how much things have changed since you lived in Haiti," I said, privately thinking that Alex needed the update as much as his part.

I suggested that he make a mental picture of himself at age

thirty-six, just as he appeared at that very moment, sitting in my apartment. He did this with some difficulty but it had the desired effect of bringing his awareness to the present.

"Now, show this picture of yourself to the part, and let it know that it's been twenty-seven years since you were a boy in Haiti. Tell the part that you live in Canada now, that you have your own apartment and that your parents are no longer in your life."

He closed his eyes and it was quite a while before he finally opened them.

"How did the part respond?" I prompted.

"It doubts I could have lived this long."

"Well, please assure it that you are still very much alive, and that a lot has changed over the years."

"It wants to know why it should believe me."

"I guess there's no reason why the part should take your word for it," I conceded. "Ask it if it would like to find out for itself what the truth is."

I suggested that he invite the part to come out of his body onto his hand. That way, it could take a good look at my apartment, at me and at Alex.

He held out his upturned palm and the part made its appearance, so to speak. I noticed that he kept his hand high and well away from his body.

"How does the part respond to what it sees?"

"It thinks this must be some kind of trick."

"Well, tell it to have a good look around. Why not take it to the window and show it the street below. Point out the makes and models of the cars."

Alex got up and went to the window.

"Ask the part: Does that look like the Haitian village where it believes you are still living?"

"No."

Alex returned to his seat, keeping his upturned palm extended.

"Tell the part to take a good look at you, Alex. Let it see for itself that you have indeed managed to live to the age of thirty-six, though your life is now in danger. Does the part know that you've been ill?"

"No, I don't think it does."

This was an interesting point, given that this part had come forward when we asked who was in charge of Alex's cancer. I asked him to remind the part of this fact, and to fill it in on what he had gone through in the past year.

"Give it all the details—your diagnosis, treatment, and what the doctors have told you about your chances for survival. Tell the part that you want to live and that's why you're having this conversation with it right now."

Alex laughed nervously as he reported the part's answer. "It says that, as far as it's concerned, I should have died years ago."

I decided to overlook this for the moment, thinking that it might be related to the secret, which would come out soon enough. Allowing the part to return to its place inside Alex I sensed that we were on much firmer ground. In spite of the part's fatalism, it clearly felt safer knowing that Alex had survived into adulthood. I did notice, though, that from this point onward the part (Alex) began sneaking furtive glances at me. Evidently, it still believed that I was trying to trick it and wanted to keep an eye on me. But there was no doubt that the update had steadied it, and Alex was now able to tell me the story of the tree with a minimum of agitation.

As a boy in Haiti, he said, he had found many opportunities to gossip with the local children and their families. His father had caught him a few times and the punishment was severe, but this didn't stop him. He was intrigued and thrilled by the villagers' stories—so unlike the boring Bible stories he heard at home. His parents didn't know that he was almost as well versed in the local customs as the village children themselves.

By the age of nine he had developed a fascination for a sacred tree that stood just beyond the village. According to local tradition the tree held special powers; it was off-limits to everyone but the voodoo doctor who used it in his rituals. In fact, the entire clearing in which the tree stood was the voodoo doctor's exclusive domain. This sacred territory was guarded only by the fear and respect it aroused in the villagers.

On many occasions Alex and the village children had sneaked into the forest to look at the tree. They always kept a safe distance, not even entering the clearing, but enjoyed alarming one another with accounts of what happened to those who defied the voodoo doctor. This powerful sorcerer, they said, knew everything that happened without having to be told and spared no one who went against him. His curses (so the story went) were so powerful they could cause agonizing deaths, even at great distances.

Alex was as much in awe of the voodoo doctor as were his young friends, even though he heard quite a different story at home. His parents had nothing but disdain for the local traditions, assuring him that voodoo was pure pagan superstition. Furthermore, they said, it was wrong to believe in it because that meant you were breaking faith with Christ.

As Alex grew older he began to echo his parents' sentiments, telling himself that the villagers were primitive and their magic bogus. He spent more and more time with the missionaries' children and even began to gather with them in small groups to poke fun at the villagers.

One evening he slipped out of the house at dusk. Skirting the village to avoid being seen he headed through the forest for the sacred tree. He had never been to the clearing alone and when he got there was dismayed to find that the fading light gave it an unusually eerie atmosphere. He looked nervously around and had to force himself to carry on. Taking a deep breath, he flung himself at the massive tree and scrambled upwards into its highest branches. Once there, a sense of gloating satisfaction came over him. He had climbed the forbidden tree and nothing bad was happening to him.

Little did he know what inner torment awaited him. That night as he lay in bed his imagination churned up all his old fears. In the shadowed darkness of his bedroom, he simply couldn't believe that he had dared to defy the voodoo doctor. He felt certain that retribution would be swift and deadly.

Relating these events, Alex sat perfectly still, staring straight ahead as if watching vivid retakes of every scene. When he came to the end of his story, a shudder went through him and he sank into his chair with a worried look.

So this was the part's secret, and this was why it believed that Alex should be long dead. When I asked the part how the secret was connected to Alex's cancer, it answered ominously, "This is the curse and you can't stop it."

"Do you believe in the power of voodoo?"

"Of course. The natives are evil pagans but their magic works."

Alex admitted that he agreed with his part, particularly as there had been many unexplained deaths in the village. He recalled a local man who had become paralyzed with pain for no apparent reason. A mission nurse went to see him but couldn't find anything wrong. After weeks of suffering the man finally choked to death on his own saliva.

"And what about you, Alex?" I pressed. "Consciously, do you believe that you have cancer because the voodoo doctor put a curse on you?"

He shrugged and looked at his hands. "Probably not."

"Ask your part this," I said. "If the voodoo doctor put a curse on Alex when he was nine, how has he managed to survive this long?"

The part had no ready answer — it had, after all, been unaware till now of Alex's true age. But the part's conviction that Alex was cursed remained unshakable. I was intrigued by its adamancy on this point and began to wonder if it might have some personal stake in Alex's death.

"Ask the part how it feels about Alex's predicament. Would it like to help him throw off this so-called curse?"

Alex dropped his head to converse inwardly with his part. When he looked up I saw that his face had gone pale.

"What did it say?"

He spoke in a whisper. "It said that I deserve to die."

This was not a great surprise from my point of view, but Alex was not prepared for it. I asked the part what Alex had done to deserve such retribution, but it was silent on this point.

"Isn't death a rather harsh punishment for a little boy who has merely followed his natural curiosity and who hasn't really done any harm?"

No answer.

"Did you hear Alex say that he doesn't believe he is cursed?"

At this, the part told us flatly that Alex had no knowledge or authority in such matters and that it didn't care what he thought.

The pieces of the puzzle were coming together in my mind. I could see that Alex had been influenced at a young age by two very different yet equally powerful religious teachings and had split (quite literally) into two minds on the subject of religious doctrine. And yet, the single overriding concept that had taken hold of him was the inevitability of punishment. If you did something wrong, you would be punished. Punishment was the one thing you could count on in life and it was sure to be harsh. This principle, which he had learned first from his father, had been confirmed by his boyhood friends in their fear of the voodoo doctor. But it was only the voodoo side of him, I thought, that seemed to expect the death penalty. Given this, and knowing that Alex's conscious commitment was to Christianity, I decided to have a go at challenging the part's belief in voodoo.

I began by pointing out that religious dogma could sometimes invoke the power of suggestion, especially when it came to the inexperienced and naive minds of children. Maybe this so-called curse was a good example of that.

"Could it be possible that Alex's devotion to the teachings of Jesus makes him more powerful than this voodoo curse, which could be entirely power of suggestion?"

The part's reply was well considered. "The Haitians worship the devil," it said. "They invoke Satan's power to work their spells and curses."

Deciding not to debate the accuracy of this statement, I asked him instead where he had learned this.

"My father told me," he answered.

I wasn't surprised that the devil had finally made an appearance, given Alex's fundamentalist heritage.

"And who do you believe is more powerful — God or Satan?"

I waited for the answer, almost certain that Satan would come out on top. In this part's cosmology, I thought, Satan is probably a variation of the all-powerful voodoo doctor. The part took its time answering, clearly giving the question some serious thought.

"God has got to be the most powerful force in the universe, but Satan can sabotage just about any good that God can do. Satan sneaks in when God isn't looking."

"When is God not looking?" I asked. "Isn't God everywhere at all times?"

"Well, yes, but Satan is tricky and God can't always stop him."

Alex looked rather pleased with this exchange. By this time the conversation was flowing easily and I could see that he had a strong rapport with this fatalistic part of himself that so feared and respected the forces of evil.

"What does the part believe about God's love?" I asked.

"God loves those who are good."

"Does the part think that Alex is good?"

"No."

I already knew that the part wanted to punish Alex but now I began to see why. It wasn't just for his misdeeds—things like climbing the tree and disobeying his parents. The part believed that Alex deserved punishment because he was fundamentally a bad person.

"What is it about Alex that makes him not good?"

The part was mysteriously silent on this point.

"You know, little boys can't be expected to have a whole lot of worldly knowledge. Doesn't God love us enough to make sure that these so-called curses can't stick on little children, who don't always make the right choices?"

"Satan doesn't care."

"Does God care?"

No answer.

"Exactly how is it that Alex is not good?" I persisted.

Alex fidgeted with his ring and didn't answer. I had to really coax him to tell me what he was thinking and he finally reported a long-forgotten memory. One morning, he said, his mother had come into his bedroom and caught him touching himself "down there." Bursting into tears, she had called her husband to the scene. The preacher had delivered a stern lecture on Satan's evil powers, and then wrapped Alex's hands in gauze and tape, leaving them bandaged for the rest of the day.

Alex blushed as he related these events. When I asked his part what decision it had made as a result of the experience, it said, "Alex is bad."

Having come this far, Alex ventured to tell me that he still felt guilty whenever he "indulged" himself. I pointed out that masturbation, whether for children or adults, was no longer considered a bad thing—in fact, most psychologists believed it to be a normal and healthy part of life. Alex wanted to know if these were Christian psychologists.

"Some of them are. Not all Christians are against masturbation."

"Well, they're not my dad's kind of Christians. But then, I don't
know if I am either."

This was the first hint I'd had that Alex's Christian doctrine
might in any way differ from what had been taught to him by his
parents. I invited him to amplify on his statement and was
rewarded by the news that he had been "born again" a few years
back. He had believed at the time that Jesus had cleared him of all
his previous sins.

"I honestly thought that I'd started on a new footing then."

I asked his part if it was listening. Did it know that Alex had
renewed his faith in recent years and that his sins had been forgiven? The part said that it knew, but argued that Alex had
embraced Jesus out of fear, not love, and so it didn't count.

I was interested to hear this part use the word love, since I so
far had the impression that the only emotions it knew were fear
and guilt. I asked it for its definition of love and was not surprised
when it said that "love means fear and obedience." It had learned
this from the Bible.

"Do you believe in the Bible?" I asked.

"Yes!" Emphatically.

"So by the definition understood from the Bible — that love is
fear and obedience — Alex did in fact embrace Jesus out of love."

I meant this to unsettle the part and it did. Alex frowned and
said that the part was confused.

"Do you sometimes, somehow feel that love might be something other than fear and obedience?"

"Yes," the part admitted.

I asked Alex what his own experience of love had been. He had
once been in love, he said, but it hadn't worked out, and now he
couldn't say that he really loved anyone.

"What about your parents?" I asked. "Did you love them? Did

they love you?"

"I don't think they loved me. I was always disappointing them. I never lived up to their expectations."

He had feared his father's anger and hated his strictness in enforcing rules. His mother had been weak—whatever she may have felt, she had never dared to intervene.

"Do you know something about love other than what your part learned from the Bible?"

When he'd been born again, he said, he had felt Jesus as a warm, forgiving presence right inside the core of himself. He put his hand to his heart. Since the onset of his cancer he had all but forgotten about that warmth, but now he had no trouble summoning it up again. We asked his part if it too could feel this different kind of love—but it had no idea what we were talking about. I encouraged Alex to fill it in.

"Invite the part to visit this energy source that you have right inside your core. Let it feel for itself what this warm, forgiving kind of love is like."

As Alex sat there with his eyes closed and his hands curled loosely in his lap, he seemed relaxed and peaceful for the first time that day. But after some minutes he looked up with a mournful shake of his head.

"What happened?" I prompted. "What does your part think about this different kind of love?"

"It can tell that it's real. The part can't deny that."

I waited for him to continue but he fell silent.

"Has the part discovered something?"

He was fidgeting again and took his time answering. When he finally did speak, his voice was filled with emotion.

"It's just that it—the part can't believe I'm worthy of that kind of love."

"Hmm. Well, we know that your part believes you're bad," I reflected. "Maybe it's time we asked it to itemize everything it finds you guilty of. If we had the whole list of sins and misdeeds then we'd know exactly what we're dealing with."

I said this fully expecting that the part would not be able to come up with much, and I was right. Examining its record of Alex's transgressions, it could list only a half dozen examples of childish disobedience.

"Do you honestly believe that children are born knowing right from wrong?" I asked it. "Isn't growing up a process of learning from experience?"

"He did things he was told not to do. He hasn't honored his parents."

I pointed out that Jesus had forgiven Alex's sins.

"He disobeyed the Ten Commandments. The law of Moses precedes the law of Jesus."

For once, I was grateful for the hours I'd spent as a child memorizing the Catholic catechism.

"Doesn't the first commandment say: Thou shalt have no other gods before me?"

"Yes."

"Are you yourself obeying that commandment when you give power to the curse of a voodoo doctor?"

The part was taken aback by this but it quickly rallied. "He lied to his parents," it said — a weak rebuttal but it wasn't giving up easily.

As the repartee continued, I asked the part why it thought that Alex deserved to die. Even if he had disobeyed his parents and even if he had lied to them, was this really terrible enough to warrant a death sentence?

The part's reply was strategic. Alex needed to be punished for his own good. He was bad and would therefore be sent to hell when he died. But if he could be sufficiently punished before he died, maybe God would take mercy on him and not send him there. Cancer was the chance Alex needed. If it was painful enough and prolonged enough, it might save him from the greater suffering he would endure in hell.

The part had taken on Alex's eternal salvation as a personal responsibility, since it couldn't risk leaving it to mere chance. What would become of him if he died quickly and painlessly in a car accident or passed on peacefully in his sleep?

This at least reflected what I knew about parts—their reasoning tends to be narrow and short-sighted, and when they set about solving problems they usually end up making a worse mess of things. But they do have our best interests at heart.

I began to question the part about its conception of God. When had it decided that God was angry and unyielding? What did God look like? How did he spend his time? As the part answered these questions it soon became apparent (to me, at least) that its picture of God was directly modeled on Alex's father. Notwithstanding the addition of a few supernatural powers, God looked, spoke and behaved like the all-too-human missionary.

I asked the part if it gave higher authority to God or to Alex's father. It wasn't sure, Alex admitted. It couldn't really distinguish between the two. After this, the part was no longer certain whether it believed in the vindictive God that resembled Alex's father or the loving divinity that Alex had embraced when he was born again.

Sensing that the part's universe had been sufficiently shaken loose, I decided that it was probably ready for a psychic-emotive release. Accordingly, I asked it to take a good look inside itself and tell me how much of what it found there belonged to Alex's father. With a little nudging it was able to identify within itself many of the father's patterns—his rigid thinking, the stern way he spoke, his inability to forgive. Since these things were acquired and had not originated with Alex, I explained, the part could release them if it so desired.

"Would you like to let it all go?" I prompted.

The part was slow to respond, not happy with the prospect of such radical change. I coaxed it gently along, emphasizing that the father's punishing mindset was shutting out the healing love that Alex so badly needed. Then I reminded it that if Alex were to die, it would die too.

"You've seen that you're a part of him. Do you think you could survive without him?"

At this, the part finally decided to proceed. Once it got started it had no trouble releasing all it could find in itself of Alex's father, including his words and gestures, and even the leather strap that he had wielded in punishment. It further agreed to clear out the whole voodoo curse, which, it discovered, consisted largely of imaginary horrors. Alex visualized this as an oozing black slime leaving his body. The relief brought by the exercise was apparent in the softening of his features. When I asked him how he felt, he said, "Weird, but better."

With the clutter gone the part was able to remember something of its larger role and purpose in Alex's life. As a boy, it said, Alex was often in trouble. His father administered harsh punishments, always accompanied by a stern lecture. I got the feeling that the lectures were the most destructive part of the discipline — delivered with fanatical righteousness, they filled the boy with devastating guilt and fear. Attempting to cope with these emotions, the part decided to soak up the father's beliefs and values so it could use them as guidelines to keep Alex out of trouble. In this way it hoped to preserve him from further punishment.

I thought this strategy was a clever one and said so to the part. But I also pointed out that it had ultimately backfired. Over the years its agenda had shifted. The part itself had become the tyrant in Alex's life — the internalized will of the father that took over the job of administering punishment. By constantly reminding him that he was bad it had ensured that he lived a life of quiet inner agony. It was satisfied knowing that he was unhappy and thus being sufficiently punished.

I asked Alex how things had changed at the time of his religious conversion. With the sense of being loved and forgiven, he said, he managed to get out from under the part's domination. Yet, he had never been able to shake the nagging feeling that he wasn't really worthy of love, and eventually the part once again got the better of him. Now, he felt that some of that "inner darkness" had been cleared away.

But even as he told me that he felt better he stared bleakly at his hands. With some gentle probing I discovered what the problem was. He didn't want to believe that his "inner darkness" arose entirely from within himself. Rather, he preferred to think of it as the work of Satan.

"What do you believe about Satan?" I asked.

He looked up and his eyes glazed over. "Satan is real. If you don't take him seriously, you're vulnerable to his influence."

It took me a moment to digest this. Finally, I said, "So you think you have to believe in him in order to protect yourself from him."

"You mean you don't believe in him?" He threw me a look of astonishment.

Knowing that I was treading on thin ice, I composed my reply carefully. "I can be open minded about it. But I'm wondering if believing in Satan and fearing him gives him more power than he would otherwise have."

At this, Alex stared at me open-mouthed. I think it was the first time that day that he actually looked me full in the face. "You sound like one of those new-agers," he said.

When I asked him how he meant that, he said, "It's naive to assume you can protect yourself from evil simply by not believing in it."

I resisted the temptation to engage him in a lengthy discussion on this subject. It was obvious that he was not going to be argued out of his attachment to Satan. And yet, I was concerned that his belief in an evil power greater than himself would inhibit his ability to heal.

By now I was fully aware that Alex had come to the session with a very limited concept of what it might take to heal himself. His idea of what cherished beliefs might come into question was nil before this moment, and he clearly took no pleasure in the insights he was gaining into himself and his illness. In fact, he seemed increasingly disturbed. Maybe he had been hoping that I would simply recite a magic spell over him and make his cancer go away. I'm certain that if he'd been given the option of living on in good health with his inner turmoil intact he would have jumped at the chance. Yet, although his resistance was consider-able, I had to acknowledge that the session was moving along reasonably well.

I took a minute to look over my notes and figure out where to go from here. The key to his part, as I saw it, was its core belief that Alex was bad and deserved to be punished. This was the deep and so-far-unshakable conviction that gave the part its rationale for wanting him dead. Yet I doubted that Alex had come into this world believing he was bad.

I asked the part to recollect its early years, to remember back before it had climbed the tree, before it had taken on the father's beliefs in order to save Alex from punishment, before it had expe-rienced any punishment.

"Can you recall a time before you decided that Alex was a bad person?"

Fully expecting more objections and delays, I was pleased when it promptly came up with the memory of a warm, comfortable, floating feeling.

"Do you know where you are?"

The part didn't know where it was. Everything was blackness.

"Hmm. Well, do you sense that you are alone? Is anyone else there with you?"

Alex looked puzzled, and then suddenly exclaimed, "Mother is there!" After a pause, he asked tentatively, "Could it be that—I mean, is it possible that the part is, uh, inside Mother?"

"Let's ask it: Does it feel like it's inside Mother?"

"It's in her womb," he said, shifting uncomfortably.

I asked the part to spend some time exploring. I wanted to know about its experience back there in the womb—how it felt and what it thought of Alex. After a pause it reported that it felt warm and safe and that it liked Alex.

"What kind of person do you think Alex is?"

Hesitating, it finally said that it had no opinion of him one way or another.

I found this gratifying considering the part's venom up till now. It wasn't saying Alex was good but it was no longer saying he was bad. To have no opinion could signify a simple, uncritical acceptance, and for a moment or two I thought we were home free. Then Alex volunteered the information that his part could see a white light.

White light is a common enough symbol and one that usually signifies a very pure state of consciousness. Yet something told me to approach this particular white light with caution.

"Ask the part what the light means."

"It's an angel."

"What does it mean to see an angel?"

"It's there to protect me."

"Protect you from what?"

"I don't know. It just feels like there's something bad that it has to protect me from."

I indulged an internal sigh. The badness was still with us after all—though at least it was no longer attached to the part.

"Can the part see where this bad something is coming from?"

Alex shook his head. "It's surrounded by darkness," he said. Then he looked up. "It couldn't be my father, could it?"

"I don't know. Ask the part."

He moved restlessly in his chair. After a while I asked him what was happening and got one of those hooded glances in reply. He fussed and fidgeted for several more minutes, and then suddenly lifted his head and gave me a long intense stare.

"You can't even be sure that angel is not Satan in disguise," he declared.

I had dared to hope that Satan was behind us. Now that the part was back in the womb, not even born into the world, how much could it know about evil? I half suspected that Alex was intentionally throwing a wrench into the works, but deciding not to jump to conclusions I asked him if he could tell where the thought of Satan had come from? Was it his own thought? Or had it come from the part, from the angel, from the darkness that the angel was protecting him from, or from somewhere else? It seemed to be coming from the darkness, he answered, and yet it was also coming from the angel.

"But it can't be the angel," he protested. "I don't want it to be the angel."

The angel and the darkness were bound up together and Alex was so distraught about this that I tried to help him separate the two. We worked at it for some time but had no success.

"Let's try something else," I suggested. "Ask your part to examine the darkness—look at it, listen to it—and see if it comes to you what belief or thought is holding it in place."

Alex dropped his head to concentrate. After a long silence, he looked up and announced: "For every good there is an equal and corresponding evil."

Now this was interesting. Back here in the womb, even though the part had not yet come to see Alex as bad, it had somehow learned this maxim about good and evil. And if, for this part, life must inevitably present something evil along with every good, then it made perfect sense that the darkness and the angel would be inseparable.

"Ask the part where it learned this rule—that for every good there is an equal evil."

"It says this in Genesis."

"And how did the part know what it says in Genesis when you were floating warm and safe in your mother's womb?"

He looked at me quizzically. "I don't know."

"Well, let's check it out. Ask the part to concentrate on its surroundings—to feel and sense everything that's going on around it."

"It hears a droning sound," Alex reported. "It sounds like a voice."

The part couldn't make out any words but when I asked if it recognized the voice Alex sank into his chair, and then suddenly sat up straight. "It's my father's voice," he said. "It's my father reading to my mother. He's reading to her from the Bible."

"Ask the part how it feels when it hears that droning intonation of Alex's father reading to Mother."

The part still felt warm and safe, said Alex, but now there was a tinge of fear and discomfort. "It just seems that when he reads to her from the Bible she feels—well, she feels guilty."

"Can the part sense what she's feeling guilty about?"

He was silent for what seemed like several minutes and when he answered he blushed. "She feels guilty about—what she had to do to bring me here."

It seemed that the womb had not been as safe and comfortable as the part had originally surmised. As I probed more deeply into its experience there, a disturbing story unfolded. Alex's parents had shared a belief that sex was unholy. Accordingly, they approached baby-making as a duty—something that had to be done and should not be enjoyed – but even so they felt guilty about it, and somehow the burden of their guilt had fallen on Alex's mother. Maybe she was the one who most wanted a child, or possibly she had expressed some tenderness or pleasure in the act of lovemaking. In any case, since her shame had come about from bringing Alex into the world, he felt that not only was he tainted and dirty like her—he was the one responsible for her fall from grace.

"That must be why he read to her from the Bible so much, especially during her pregnancy," Alex speculated. "It was his way of trying to cleanse her of her sin."

I asked the part what had made the greater impression on it—the actual words that Father had read, his tone of voice and manner of reading, or what Mother was feeling when he read to her.

"It was the way he read and how she felt—sometimes good and sometimes not so good."

She felt good, the part explained, because she was getting some positive attention from her husband in a way that did not go against her beliefs. And she felt not so good because when he got that stern, preachy tone that sounded like God talking, she remembered the bad thing she had done to conceive a child.

This, at least, was the part's story. Alex said he had no idea how his part could know these things, adding that he couldn't be sure any of it was true. And yet, some of the details struck a chord in his conscious memory. He recalled, for example, that he had always hated it when his father read from the Bible, feeling that he and his mother were meant to endure it as a penance.

I told him that I thought the story made sense considering that for as long as he could remember he had felt that he was a bad person. Even in the womb he'd been drawn into the painful web of his parents' prohibitive beliefs. His very entry into the world had made him an accomplice in their guilt and in the tension that grew up between them because of it. His mother had taken the role of supplicant, his father the duty of absolving her, and little Alex was left with the feeling that he was the cause of it all. Nurtured over the years by his father's stern lectures and harsh punishments, the belief that he was bad had gradually assumed a life of its own.

Alex could see how the belief in his own badness had fallen into place in those early, formative days and how he and his part had been working at cross purposes, especially since the onset of his cancer. With this powerful aspect of his own nature determined to punish him, he'd been up against tremendous odds in his efforts to get well.

I reminded him that we had started on this entire area of exploration because we were unable to separate the angel from the darkness.

"What has become of the angel," I asked. "Is it still there?"

He closed his eyes; then shook his head. "It's gone. I can't see it anywhere."

At this he looked extremely distraught. He had regarded the angel as a sign that there was at least some goodness and rightness in him.

"Without it, what hope do I have?"

I commented that it was the angel who had led him to these important new insights and that may have been its reason for appearing—but this failed to have the comforting effect I intended. He could only shake his head forlornly and say that with the angel gone the surrounding darkness was more oppressive than ever.

"Take a look at that darkness," I urged. "Can you describe it?"

The darkness was a thick, cloying fog of fear and doom. It was suffocating, he said, but he couldn't throw it off.

He did indeed appear choked with misery, pale and taut like a frightened child.

When I asked him to check the fog for sounds and images he found it alive with evil spirits. On closer inspection the spirits became an angry God, which then turned into an image of his father mouthing predictions of doom. He could hear the preacher's voice raised in stern, punishing tones and the sound of his mother weeping. He knew that these sounds and images were merely echoes of a dark past, and yet he couldn't help but feel completely overwhelmed by them.

I thought it was time for another psychic-emotive release and said, "How would you feel if you thought you could shake off this fog for good?"

He looked at me as if startled and said, "That's impossible." Then, to my surprise he launched into a brief but bitter tirade.

"Maybe you've helped me discover some of the things that are wrong with me and that are making me sick, but what good does it do? I'm going to die anyway and the only thing that's changed is now I really know how rotten I am inside."

I sat staring at him for a moment before I found my voice.

"That may be true," I agreed tentatively. "But at least you now also know that the fear and doom and everything rotten that makes up the darkness doesn't even belong to you."

"What difference does that make? I'm stuck with it."

"Why not ask your part if it can lift up a corner of that darkness and take a look underneath."

Although Alex remained scornful, his part agreed to try this, and to his amazement (and my relief), it found that underneath the darkness there was light. It was the same light that the angel had been made of, only now it was everywhere—a soft, all-pervasive glow. The transformation was dramatic. Alex seemed to glow with ecstasy. The angel's whole purpose in appearing to him, he said, had surely been to lead him to this place. There was no badness anywhere and the darkness he had left behind already seemed insignificant.

So insignificant that he wanted to sail right on into the light without a backward glance and without finishing the job of house-cleaning that we had begun. I knew that it would not be enough to simply put the darkness behind him. He needed to go through the ritual of sending it out of his mind and body, along with all the thoughts, words and deeds that it was made of. I reigned him in until he completed this task, and then let him continue into the light, which he did with unbridled enthusiasm.

"Can you tell how far the light reaches?" I asked. "Is there anything beyond it?"

"The light goes on forever," he said. "It has no boundaries."

"What is the part feeling now that it's in this light?"

"It feels like it belongs here. It's just part of the light."

"As part of the light, what does it feel about Alex?"

"Alex is good."

Considering that the part's lifelong mission had been to punish Alex for his badness, this was music to my ears.

"What does the light itself feel like to the part?" I asked.

Alex's gaze turned inward. Somehow, I knew before he spoke what his answer would be.

"Love," he said. "It's a feeling of—just this—incredible love."

"Can the part sense where the love is coming from?"

"It's all around. The light is love."

His eyes shone and he seemed alive with radiant energy. I understood the state he was in to be a completely natural one—an original awareness that we all have within us. I had witnessed it many times before and was delighted that Alex had tapped into it, yet something told me that this rollover had its limitations.

"In the love that's all around and that you're a part of," I continued, "what do you feel and sense about God?"

"God is here. The love is God." Alex spoke reproachfully, as though this was something any child would know.

"Okay, well, ask your part: In this love that is God and that you're part of, do you feel that God loves you?"

He hesitated. "I don't know. How can I be sure?"

"Ask him."

There was a long silence. "Yes. God loves me."

"And do you love God?"

"Of course."

"So then, if God loves you and you love God, and you are part of the loving light, which is God, would it feel right for you to say the words, I love me?"

In his peaceful, glowing state, he seemed to take this in and find it acceptable. His radiance remained undiminished as he turned the phrase over in his mind, his lips vaguely forming the words. But then his face clouded over.

"No," he said. "That would be blasphemy."

This was more or less what I'd expected, knowing that many old-fashioned fundamentalist Christians consider self-love to be the worst form of pride. But I was not willing to give up too easily and asked him to tune in to the God whom he loved and who loved him.

"How would this God feel about Alex if he loved himself?"

After a moment's reflection he said that it would seem normal and right—just the way of things. But when it came to actually saying the words, he couldn't do it. Even though his part was experiencing an all-encompassing, limitless love, his conscious mind would not allow this boundary to be erased.

I felt that if Alex could fully embrace the love he had found, his chances for healing would be greatly enhanced. I wanted to push him but knew that I must back off. He had not given me the authority to challenge his religious beliefs and besides, fighting his resistance would likely end up magnifying it. Alex believed that he was loved by a compassionate God and he accepted as new beliefs, *I am good* and *I am loved*. Incomplete by my standards, but it would have to do.

As we neared the end of our session my main concern was whether his part, which had claimed responsibility for giving him cancer in the first place, could now reverse the process and begin the work of healing. I asked it to remain where it was in the loving light and look forward in time to the place where Alex floated in his mother's womb.

"Take a look at the baby's developing body. Is it healthy?"

The part described the body as strong, full of vitality and capable of healing any illness that might arise. When I asked if it could bring that original healing ability into the body of the thirty-six-year-old Alex, it was hesitant. The part wanted to cooperate but didn't think it could do this.

"I don't know if God loves me enough."

Both Alex and his part maintained that health was a gift from God, not something they could choose. The only way he could regain his health, said Alex, would be if God made a point of singling him out for healing, and he did not think this likely.

I asked the part to look again at its experience of God from within the light and to compare that with what it had learned about God from Alex's father.

"Which of these impressions of God would give you the right to ask for healing?"

It was obvious, Alex said with a glance.

"Would the part like to ask God for healing?"

He flushed and didn't answer.

"Does this part want Alex to live?"

Again, no answer.

"Alex, do you want to live?"

"Yes, but—"

"Ask the part if it cares what Alex wants."

"Only if it's what God wants."

I led the part once again through an exploration of the light and the unbounded love it had found there.

"Ask the love energy if it wants Alex to live."

"Yes. Maybe."

"Make sure."

"Yes. It wants me to live."

"Alex, would you be willing to trust the love and ask it to help you bring back the ability to your mind and body to heal your illness?"

Alex's eyes filled with tears, which he quickly wiped away. When I asked him what he was feeling, he said, "I don't know if it's too late."

"Well, let's keep an open mind. You've discovered some goodness right inside the core of yourself and you know that God loves you and that you love God. At least your part has the energy it needs to give it a try."

He was really crying now and I steadied him as best I could. When his tears subsided, I asked him how strongly he could believe in the warm, compassionate, all-loving and all-accepting energy that his part had discovered.

"It could be the beginning of you healing yourself."

"I don't know if I have the faith."

"Would you like this part to help you with your faith?"

"Yes."

Knowing that he would need every inner resource he could muster to help him through the time ahead, whether it ended in healing or in death, I asked him to call up the warm, compassionate love that he had felt when he was born again, and to join that with the energy of the light. The two energies were essentially the same and came together easily.

Now I spoke to his part, directing it to bring the love forward through time. This was important. The part felt good while it remained in the light but I knew that its negative beliefs would resurface if I allowed it to return unaltered to the present. I wanted it to use the love energy to actually transform the many destructive beliefs it had taken on throughout the course of Alex's life.

"Let the warm, loving, compassionate energy of the light come forward through time, and as it comes forward, allow it to dissolve the whole group of beliefs that Alex is a bad person—

that he is guilty for being a product of sex, that he is bad for touching himself, bad for climbing the tree, bad for not living up to his parents' expectations, and doomed to die as punishment for his sins."

The part readily let go of its negative attitudes about Alex, but when it came to the belief that self-love is blasphemous, it (Alex) was unwilling to budge. When I further suggested that it consider dissolving its belief in Satan's power, Alex glared his disapproval, letting me know that his religious doctrine was not open for debate.

"After all," he argued, "this whole process could be a trick of the devil."

"Do you believe it is?"

"I sure hope not."

I smiled and said that I didn't think he needed to worry, considering that throughout the session we had focused entirely on discovering the goodness in him. I did realize, though, that in Alex's mind Satan had the power to sabotage all that we had accomplished, to flood his awareness with renewed thoughts of fear and doom and shroud him once again in darkness.

I asked him to check with his part now that it had brought the love energy all the way to the present. The warm glow that reappeared on his face told me that the love he had found was at least as solid and real to him as Satan was. This love was what we had to work with and I knew that we had to make it good—to somehow ensure that its power would triumph. I spoke to the part, asking what it could do to help Alex now that it was filled with love.

After a moment's thought Alex answered with a pleased look. "The part says it can keep God with me."

I spent some time affirming the part in this new role. Bringing God's love to Alex, it agreed, was an innate talent that it had somehow lost along the way. Now that it had recovered this talent, it would not forget about it again.

"Did the part hear Alex talking about his belief in Satan?"

"Yes."

"How does it feel about Satan's power? Could Satan influence it in any way?"

After a few long moments, during which Alex must have carefully assessed the strength of both the god and the devil within him, he looked up and said, "God can withstand anything Satan might try to do to him."

As he got up to leave he told me that he would have a lot to think about over the next while. I suggested that he might benefit from another session and invited him to call me if he felt the need, but I didn't hear from him again.

———————

For some months I cherished a private hope that Alex had started on the road to recovery. When I think of Alex today, however, I no longer imagine that he survived his illness — or if I do, it is only in moments of self-indulgence.

In the years since our session I've gained more experience with diseases that are believed to be terminal. On the whole I've found them to be complex and many layered — just what you might expect from years of nurturing fears and suppressing vital emotions at subconscious levels, as Alex had done. Working with such diseases on a psychological basis requires a committed effort — and yet I've often found that those who have such diseases are impatient and unwilling to follow through. Like Alex, they usually seek me out only because they are desperate and vulnerable, and they often harbor a mixture of hope, cynicism and disbelief that make progress difficult.

It goes without saying that our spiritual beliefs and orientation can deeply affect our well being. Alex's discovery of the light was—for me, as for him—a great moment in our session. In all of my experiments I have consistently found light under darkness and it may be this self-discovered truth that has kept me going over the years. But Alex's landscape of darkness and doom was so pervasive that I really didn't know if he would be able to get through it and beyond it. Normally, the darkness would have been cleared out in advance of finding the light. To "cheat" by lifting up a corner was simply to see if there was something promising underneath. We were lucky. We could have found more of the same or worse. But once found, the light provided the resource needed to cope with the darkness.

The most difficult problem Alex presented was that he had lost all hope. He simply did not believe it possible that he could get well again. I agree that, from the perspective of medical science, he probably had no chance at all—his doctors had never seen anyone recover from what he had. But I also know that all of us have powerful resources that we seldom use or even think about in connection with a health crisis.

Love is the most powerful healing energy available to us. Almost everyone has some experience of the universe of possibility that is opened by love. When we love and feel loved, the body relaxes, the immune system does its work and our whole inner environment becomes supportive and regenerative. Alex came very close to being able to utilize this natural force—first with his experience of being reborn, and again with the discovery of his inner light. He found love but he could not fully reconcile it with what he had been taught to believe. Layering new beliefs over old ones is not usually very effective, which is why affirmations have limited power.

If there had been further opportunities to work with Alex, to build trust between us, we might have been able to integrate his experience of love more fully. As things stood I'm not certain how much he actually did accept. I don't think he felt that God loved him quite enough to perform a healing miracle on his behalf. And I do know that he drew a line at the idea that he could love himself.

All the same, he accomplished a lot in the hours we spent together. He examined at least one layer of his illness, transformed some powerful psychological fears, integrated his born-again experience and touched the godhead in himself. If this was not enough to cure him it did at least relieve some of his inner turmoil and allow him to believe in a God who would accept him when he died. My most realistic hope for Alex is that he met his death with inner serenity, undisturbed by a fear of hell.

What the Doctor Didn't Know (I)

Some people go through life without a day's illness; others seem to somatize all their troubles, falling ill at every sign of stress. Deanna was a member in good standing of the latter group.

She first turned up in my life as a quiet, serious presence at one of my weekend seminars. On the first morning, as everyone was getting seated, she approached me to complain that people were smoking. She asked if I would put a stop to it—otherwise she would have to leave, she explained, because she was extremely allergic to cigarette smoke. At a time when smoking was generally tolerated, her request was unusual.

Deanna's health problems were encyclopedic and her personal history was a saga of medical woes. At forty, she was still living with her parents because each time she tried to leave some new health crisis intervened. When she was twenty-two, for instance, it was exhaustion due to hypothyroid, and although her doctor put her on thyroid medication it took two years to get her dose properly adjusted. When she again began making plans to move she twisted her ankle while gardening, dislocating her knee as she fell. Surgery was required. Her leg was in a cast for two months, and after that she needed prolonged physiotherapy.

Then came the sympathectomies. The specialist who treated her knee noticed that each time she came to see him her hands and feet perspired so much that she soaked the paper on his examining table. He suggested that she see a cardiovascular and thoracic surgeon for this problem. Deanna's history of profuse sweating had already led her to have most of the sweat glands under her arms surgically removed. Now she underwent four further operations on her sympathetic nervous system. The nerves along the breast and hip bones were severed so that her hands and feet no longer received the signal to sweat. Surgical clips were inserted to keep the nerves from re-patterning.

Most disabling on an ongoing basis were her allergies. Deanna was allergic to so many foods that she had little choice but to eat some of them anyway. She couldn't tolerate alcohol or any kind of fumes, and was reactive to wool and domestic animals. She was plagued by week-long migraine headaches—her most common allergic reaction—but sometimes her symptoms were more dramatic. When she ate cheese, for example, the skin on the back of her hands split into a network of bleeding lines. Even her allergist had never seen anything like it.

She was also susceptible to infections of every kind. When a flu bug was going around she was sure to catch it—and where others might be sick for three or four days, Deanna was bedridden for several weeks. Around the time I met her she was complaining of tiredness, and her doctors had suggested that she might have chronic fatigue syndrome. Tests revealed a low white-blood-cell count, but the diagnosis was inconclusive.

I thought that Deanna must have spent half her waking hours in the company of health professionals: allergists, dermatologists, neurologists, internal specialists, orthopedic surgeons, chiropractors, physiotherapists, lab technicians and nurses. I'd be willing to bet that doctors made up most of the entries in her address book, since she had a different specialist for each of her ailments. As she herself told me, illness was the central fact that her life was built on.

It had never occurred to Deanna that illness could begin in the mind. Like her parents, her doctors and much of society, she regarded the body as a material entity requiring material remedies.

When she came to that first weekend seminar of mine it was not with any notion of restoring her health—rather, she felt that her life was getting to be a burden and was curious to find out what I had to offer. Soon after that initial seminar she took my three-week intensive, but even after such extended exposure to my ideas and methods she was slow to make a connection between her health problems and her emotional life.

At the same time, it was becoming more and more glaring to me that Deanna's physical problems had an active psychological component. As I learned about her life I began to understand where the stresses and strains lay. For one thing, she felt completely intimidated by her father, who had openly ridiculed her since childhood. She recalled, for instance, that if she was reading or doing homework, he would insist that it was unhealthy to spend so much time indoors with books. Then, in the next breath, he complained that her school marks weren't good enough. Over the long run she received the message that whatever she did was not okay, and that she herself was not okay. In my opinion, this was the core of her inner stress and her inability to become a fully functioning adult.

Deanna was not someone you would immediately peg as an invalid. Tall and stately, she had ice-blond hair, cut short, and a pale complexion. She was intelligent and self-possessed, rarely showing any sign of emotion. Even when she talked about her problems she came off as cool and level-headed, virtually unflappable. I grew to enjoy her thoughtfulness and was pleased that she continued to attend my seminars. As we got to know one another, I cautiously offered my perception that her health problems might be linked to her emotional life. Puzzled at first, she eventually observed that there were certain benefits attached to her illnesses.

"When I'm sick, Mom takes care of me and Dad keeps his distance. As long as I'm in bed he doesn't ridicule me."

I felt certain that her health would improve if she worked on it directly, and suggested that she do a process on her "health part." I thought this would be more efficient than trying to tackle each of her ailments separately. It was my guess that some overall psychological strategy was responsible for a large group of her symptoms. She was intrigued by my suggestion and said she would think about it. But it wasn't till several months later, at a practice session during one of my advanced seminars, that the right moment finally arrived.

I remember the occasion well because it took place on a sweltering day in late July when the air conditioning had broken down. As the group split into pairs and small clusters, I noticed that Deanna had teamed up with another student named Beth. I joined them briefly to see what they were up to, and they told me their plan: Beth was going to work with Deanna on her health part.

As the afternoon progressed, my time was spent helping with processes in different parts of the room. Each time I glanced over at Beth and Deanna they seemed to be working well together— Beth asking questions and taking notes, Deanna fanning herself with a notebook as she made her replies. I had no idea how it was going and did not learn anything about what happened until I spoke with them the next day. In order to reconstruct the process here, I have called on Deanna's memory as well as Beth's notes, which, thankfully, have survived.

Deanna's health part appeared to her as an engineer—"a stumpy little guy wearing a white lab coat and smoking a cigar." The part's job was to monitor the body's systems and organs; his domain was a vast control room where he kept rows of test tubes filled with "essential nutrients." By pulling on levers he could release the nutrients into the blood in amounts that registered on a series of gauges.

The part was extremely earnest and intense. "I'm in charge of the whole thing," he said, puffing on his cigar. "It's a very important job."

He complained, however, that there was too much to do.

"The allergies are the biggest pain in the ass. They take too much time to monitor because there are so many."

On top of the allergies, he said, there were countless other problems to be watched.

"Such as?" Beth asked.

"The doctor says there aren't enough white blood cells."

"Have you checked on that yourself?"

"I didn't have time to do that reading. There are too many other things to think about."

The harried part was responsible not only for monitoring the body but also for keeping the control room in good working order. This, he felt, was something of a burden. He was working too hard, he was tired — and there were things that puzzled him. The extra wiring for instance.

According to the part, the safety system in the control room had somehow been bypassed and a whole new wiring system had been rigged on top of the original one.

"The extra wiring is responsible for the allergies. That much I know."

But when asked who might have tampered with the wiring, he stood there scratching his head and admitted that he had never thought about it. All he could say was that the system went into "maintenance mode" when he slept. One morning he had come on shift and found the extra wiring in place.

"When I walked in it was like a mess of monkeys had been at it."

The wiring was such a jumble that he couldn't make heads or tails of it. Now, he could no longer remember how it had looked originally, and he didn't dare try to untangle it.

"Besides, I can't find my wire cutters," he said despairingly.

Frustrated and confused, the part was not only weighed down with responsibility, he felt utterly isolated in his work. Many of the problems he was trying to cope with were beyond his understanding, and there was no one to offer help or support. Still, like most parts, he sincerely wanted to do a good job.

"If only I could restore the wiring—then everything would run a lot smoother."

Beth asked him to think back to the day he had walked in and found the extra wiring in place. At first he was perplexed, but when he gave it some thought certain things came back to him. Around that time, he recalled, Deanna had been involved in a big dispute with her parents.

"There was so much emotional stress the system went into overload and short-circuited."

Asked to amplify, he explained that the stress had driven the demand for nutrients sky high.

"The body was burning up food so fast that she couldn't eat enough to keep up. This caused the polarity to reverse on some of the circuit boards. The circuits blew and the levels on the gauges went haywire." He paused to reflect. "There are thirty gauges that monitor nutrients and I couldn't get a reliable reading off one of them. I was left with no way to monitor the body's needs."

Deanna recalled the dispute her part was referring to: "When I graduated from high school and decided that I wanted to go to university, my father did everything in his power to prevent me. He said I was too stupid to make a go of it and refused to help me financially."

A battle of wills raged until, for the first time in her life, Deanna made a decision to proceed on her own.

"I was accepted into the University of Toronto. I got a grant that covered tuition and I paid for everything else myself."

All went well for the first month or so. Then, suddenly, she began getting headaches.

"That was the beginning of the allergies, though I didn't know it at the time. I only knew that I was getting these migraines on a regular basis and missing half my classes."

She managed to pass her year, but on arriving home in the spring decided that she was too sick to go back.

"Dad said I was a failure, that I had wasted people's money. He said that women didn't need a university education, that they should be secretaries."

The engineer sighed and fretted as Deanna related this story. If only he had kept the circuits from blowing, he said, there would be no rewiring and no allergies and he wouldn't be in this mess. "All I can do now is prevent it from happening again," he said.

"How would he do that?" Beth asked.

The strategy he'd been using, he explained, was to cause a shutdown at the first sign of emotional stress.

"What do you mean by a shutdown?"

"I give her a low-grade headache or make her feel tired so she goes to bed. That way, the stress is stopped before she gets really sick."

If he left it too long, said the part, Deanna would come down with a long-term infection or one of her crippling migraines. When he let things go that far there was a real danger to the system. Unfortunately, it still happened far too often. He was so busy monitoring his gauges that he didn't always catch it in time.

Beth asked the logical question. "Isn't it up to Deanna to remove herself from stressful situations?"

But the part did not believe that she was capable of doing that, and Deanna agreed. She wasn't good at saying no. She tended to go along with whatever people expected of her. Years later, she told me this: "I had locked my emotions away in the deepest part of me, hidden even from myself. I lived as a shell, reflecting only the emotions that others wanted to see."

Because she was emotionally absent, people could walk all over her and she would not speak up on her own behalf. The only strategies she had for holding onto her identity were passive and surreptitious—getting sick, for instance, which worked well with her family. Not only did illness relieve her from doing things she didn't want to do, it got her some privacy and positive attention in an otherwise controlling and dismissive environment.

The health part, Deanna noted, followed her lead by inducing physical symptoms any time she felt stressed. It was suddenly becoming clear to her that if she could learn to be straight with people—say yes when she meant yes and no when she meant no—then the part would not have to do what it was doing. This would mean a complete turnaround in her way of interacting with people. It stood before her as a real possibility.

As Beth and Deanna continued the session, things began falling into place.

"Take another look at the extra wiring," said Beth to the engineer. "Can you see now what is holding it there?"

"The words and opinions of others," the part replied.

"Which others do you mean?"

"Doctors."

"What do you believe about the words and opinions of doctors?"

"They define you."

By this time in her life Deanna had lost much of her former devotion to doctors and had come to believe that she herself was ultimately responsible for her health. She now took the time to update her part on this change in her thinking, letting him know that he did not have to accept anyone's authority but hers, particularly in matters of health. When the part had digested this news he seemed pleased and relieved.

"So what about those words and opinions of others?" Beth asked the part. "Would you like to challenge them?"

"I would," he said with enthusiasm. And even as he thought about it, the extra wiring on his circuit boards started to come apart in his hands. Underneath, he found all his circuits in their original condition. He was pleased of course, but a little puzzled.

It had been so long since he'd seen the original system that he couldn't quite remember how it worked. He scratched his head, studied the panels and puffed on his cigar.

"I guess it's all pretty self-evident," he said at last.

"Can you tell if everything is in order?"

"Well, actually it seems to be functioning perfectly."

"And how does that affect the body?"

He paused to consider, and then said with satisfaction, "It means that the body is healthy."

Quite rightly, Beth did not accept this statement at face value. "What does good health mean to you?" she asked.

The part pondered at length. "Flexibility and resilience," he finally replied.

"So what would you do if Deanna got a headache?"

"As with any illness, the body would find it easy to rebalance itself."

"Okay, good. But let's say the doctor found a problem that needed fixing — like the previous problems that required surgery."

Deanna replied, "The part understands now that what doctors have to say is just information. It's up to me to decide what course of action I want to take."

Driving all her illnesses, she explained, had been her reliance on doctors. She had given complete authority to the medical model of illness — a system that was valid in many ways but, like any system, had its flaws.

When Beth asked the part to verbalize the truths that now seemed self-evident to him, he said: *health is a natural state ... I am healthy continuously ... I am in authority.* As Deanna repeated these phrases aloud she suddenly laughed. "All the control panels just lit up. They look exactly like the ones on the Starship Enterprise."

Meanwhile, the engineer was growing younger. His paunch was diminishing rapidly, and a thick crop of brown hair was sprouting on his head.

"How does he feel about all these changes?" asked Beth.

"He's very happy — but he's not sure what to do with himself."

Deanna explained that the control room could pretty much run itself now. With the original system back in place there were no more levers to be pulled and the gauges needed little more than an occasional check. The part had complained of overwork but he didn't want to be out of a job altogether.

"He's always admired the bridge crew that works upstairs in the brain," said Deanna thoughtfully.

"Would he like to be part of that operation?"

"He's joining them now. They're welcoming him and showing him around."

The part's new job, she said, would be to help her assess information about her health and make appropriate decisions. Whatever she decided, he would stand behind her.

It was early evening when Deanna and Beth ended the session — they had been at it for seven hours. Others in the room were also finishing up, and people were stretching their legs and talking about where to go for dinner.

An hour later Deanna, myself, and a dozen others were seated in a crowded Italian restaurant. The proprietor had put us at an L-shaped table where the general roar was deafening and a thick cloud of cigarette smoke hung in the air. Deanna was seated across from me and a few seats over. She was talking to the person next to her and seemed oddly oblivious to the smoke. Then I noticed the glass of beer in front of her. Remembering her allergy to alcohol I thought to myself, "That can't be hers." Until I saw her take a swig.

I was even more alarmed when the food arrived and she bit into slice of pizza that was literally dripping with cheese. I considered that maybe her process with Beth had gone well, but even so I thought she was pushing her luck. Leaning across the table I managed to catch her eye.

"Are you sure you should be eating that?" I had to shout to make myself heard.

"I feel fine so far," she yelled back.

Throughout the meal I waited for her to keel over, or at least get up and leave. But several hours later she was still with us. When I dropped her off at her hotel around midnight she was fine—and when I spoke to her the next day she said she had slept well and had never felt better.

Two years later, she put it this way: "Immediately after the health process my allergies disappeared completely. Cigarette smoke didn't bother me. I could drink wine and beer. I could even eat cheese. I could eat all the things I had been allergic to and nothing bothered me. I had no more migraines. None at all."

It took her longer to fully integrate what had happened.

"It turned my whole life upside-down, that seven hours. Some of the things we touched were so deep that I still don't know what I was working out. After the process I went into seclusion for a year—I craved the time by myself. I felt like a kaleidoscope that somebody had shaken—everything was settling into a totally new pattern."

During that year I spoke with her on the phone several times. At one point she told me that she had come to a new realization: She had been clinging to a childish ideal of family life, pretending to herself that her parents stood behind her. She knew now that she had to find ways to support and encourage herself, because they were not going to do that.

When she emerged from her seclusion, she picked up roots and moved west. Today, more than five years later, the allergies and headaches have not returned. Her general health has been consistently excellent, allowing her to work full time, maintain an apartment, and enjoy her independence.

It took Deanna three years from the time of our first meeting to prepare for the process on her health part. If she had tried it sooner I don't think she could have done it—she had placed too much stock in medicine and too little belief in herself. What changed that was the cumulative effect of processes she undertook in seminars, along with a growing understanding that there was more to illness than meets the eye. Over time, these things brought her to the point where she could look at her pattern and consider changing it.

Given Deanna's family life, the benefits of illness far outweighed everything else. When she was sick, her father let her be and her mother took care of her. It was a good racket—too good to give up. Until she reached the point when her life began to feel like a burden, she had no reason to look for insights or solutions.

The health process was a major turning point in Deanna's life. Not only did she begin to feel well, she lost much of her fear of life and her dependence on doctors and her parents. Prior to that she would not have considered leaving her home town because that would mean leaving her doctors. She'd spent years building up a network of specialists who understood her problems and knew which treatments helped her. Interestingly, once she did move, it was months before she remembered to sign up for health care. That's how people behave who are not worried about their health.

What the Doctor Didn't Know (II)

Two years after her allergies cleared up, Deanna approached me about working on her thyroid disorder. She had been diagnosed with hypothyroid at age twenty-two, and for twenty years had been taking medication on a daily basis. This disorder was the only medical condition that had not been resolved by her health process (see previous chapter).

The thyroid gland, located in the throat, makes two products: thyroxine and triiodothyronine, which together are known as thyroid hormone. When the gland makes too little hormone the result is hypothyroidism. Symptoms include tiredness, confusion and a slow pulse rate, or as Deanna put it: "I was constantly exhausted, often slept for twenty-four hours straight, gained weight easily, felt cold all the time and lost the ability to make decisions."

The medical solution is to provide the body with a synthetic version of thyroid hormone, which eliminates symptoms and restores energy levels to normal. Deanna (like millions of others) felt fine as long as she took her daily pill. And yet, she wasn't happy about it. She disliked having to go for a blood test every six months and she wanted to end her dependence on medication.

"I'd like to get used to my own natural rhythms," she told me. "I don't like having them forced into a pattern by a drug."

Our goal was to restore Deanna's thyroid gland to its natural optimum functioning so she could say goodbye to her pills. We decided to spend one session working directly with her thyroid, and do follow-up work if necessary. It would be important, we realized, to have the cooperation of Deanna's doctor. There would have to be blood tests before and after our session to monitor the level of thyroid hormone in her system. If we were successful, the tests would show her thyroid gland increasing its output of hormone. Her doctor could then reduce or eliminate her medication accordingly.

The first step was for Deanna to visit her doctor and explain what we had in mind. This particular doctor, a busy general practitioner, had been prescribing Deanna's thyroid medication for less than a year—only since Deanna had moved west. She was, however, aware that Deanna's condition had been stable for some twenty years, and needless to say, she was skeptical of our plan. It must have seemed to her that we were as likely to succeed if we planned to sprout wings and fly to the moon. Nonetheless, she agreed to do the tests.

Deanna and I scheduled our session for a Thursday afternoon in July. Several days before that, she went for blood test number one, which showed the expected results: Her thyroid gland was making three-quarters of what she needed and her medication was making up the remaining quarter. Thus prepared, Deanna and I embarked on our session.

I began by inquiring if she had any concerns about the work we were about to do. She assured me that she did not.

"I'll know immediately if my thyroid gland kicks in because I'll get hyper."

Hyperthyroidism results when there is too much thyroid hormone in the body. If Deanna's thyroid gland stepped up its production as we planned, she would indeed be getting too much because her daily dose of synthetic hormone would tip the balance. Her symptoms might include dizziness, diarrhea, loss of appetite and a quickened pulse. But with her doctor there to quantify changes and adjust her medication, Deanna was not concerned. Satisfied that she was ready for action, I started on the process without further ado.

"Ask inside if the part in charge of the hypothyroidism will communicate with you in consciousness."

Deanna tilted her head as if listening, and then said there were rustling noises within as all her parts turned to look at one another.

"They're trying to decide who's in charge."

After several minutes of silence I said, "Maybe they don't know. So let's ask your thyroid gland if it will talk to us directly."

She nodded, touching her throat.

We thus began our conversation with the thyroid gland, or at least with a part of Deanna's mind that was directly linked to it. When I asked the part what job it did for Deanna, it said simply that it secreted its substances into her system to give her energy.

"Is the part aware that you've been taking a synthetic supplement?"

"Yes."

"What does it think of that?"

She wrinkled her nose. "It's flat—like coffee without the kick."

"Does the part understand why you are taking this substance?"

She hesitated, closing her eyes. "It says there are too many demands on it. It can only put out so much in a day and gets tired trying to keep up."

When I asked the part what demands were placed on it, Deanna frowned. "There are words echoing in my head. Most of them sound like things Dad used to say."

"Such as?"

"Oh, you know—everybody should start work at eight o'clock in the morning … you should go to bed before eleven at night … you have to be doing something every minute of the day—things like that." She laughed. "That's my dad. It's do, do, do all the time. He used to prod me on by telling me I was a failure."

"What did he want you to be doing?"

"Dad believes you should be doing something physical, something measurable. You don't stop and think—you don't balance things. In fact, the whole thing seems designed to shut out reflection."

"Interesting. What is the feeling that goes with that kind of doing?"

She sat up straight. "A tremendous sense of urgency—because no matter how much you do, there's another job waiting."

I could see that the part had taken Dad's philosophy to heart.

"But trying to rush all the time just makes it tired," Deanna added. "As much as it dislikes the synthetic stuff, it's grateful for the help."

How appropriate, I thought, that the pressure to go faster and do more had resulted in a slowing down. The feeling of insufficiency had become literal in its effects.

"Let's ask your thyroid part: Does it have any idea what a normal amount of energy would be?"

Deanna gazed at the ceiling, and then at her hands. "It does have a picture of a more meditative lifestyle—rather than this series of urgent deadlines that it's been living with."

"What would that more meditative lifestyle be like?"

"Relaxed. Spontaneous. It would mean living according to an internal rhythm rather than an imposed one."

"Ask the part to contemplate that relaxed internal rhythm. How does it feel?"

She closed her eyes. "It feels good."

"In that picture, are things getting done or are you just doing nothing?"

"You do things but the pace is different. There's no need to rush because there's plenty of time for everything."

"Now ask this thyroid part: Do you agree with all these rules that have come down from Dad?"

"It did agree with them. It doesn't now."

Deanna had told me at the outset that she wanted to get back to her own internal rhythms. Judging by how quickly the part was learning, I gathered that her conscious clarity was having an influence on it.

This being an energy part I asked it about its concept of energy.

"There's energy in and energy out," it said. "Eating and sleeping are energy in; working is energy out."

According to the part, some activities, like thinking and walking, went both ways—involving the output of energy but also providing sustenance and renewal. The part used the energy coming in to manufacture its hormone.

"Does it believe there's enough energy coming in?"

"Yes."

"Could it produce more of its hormone, given the energy that's coming in?"

"Maybe. But it has to be careful because of the synthetic stuff I'm taking. It sees the medication as a kind of plug or stopper."

The part knew that increasing its production of hormone even slightly would make Deanna hyper. It clearly recalled the time twenty years before when Deanna had first started on thyroid medication. Initially, her doctor had given her too high a dose.

"How did that feel?" I asked.

"Like a runaway train. Because it's imposed from the outside you don't have any control over it. It's different than powering up your own natural energy."

Ever since, the thyroid had taken great care to moderate its hormone production. When I asked how it knew what amount was required, Deanna reported that it kept a series of test tubes, each marked with a red line.

"It makes enough hormone to fill each test tube to the red line. If it goes over, that's called redlining. If we start redlining, we're in trouble."

The part lived in fear of this hazard but at the same time felt constantly under pressure to produce.

"It's been hitting the gas and the brakes at the same time."

To my mind there was an element of isolation in the part's dilemma. It seemed to me that it had been stranded with too much responsibility and too little information.

"Is it aware of its relationship to the rest of your body?"

Deanna blinked. "It's never really thought about that."

I asked her to take the part on a tour through her body. It needed to see that it belonged to a wonderfully efficient system designed to balance and maintain energy levels. It was not alone; it had support.

"Introduce it to the other glands, to the organs, the bloodstream and all the chemicals that the body produces in addition to thyroid hormone. Show it the digestive chemicals, female hormones, insulin, adrenaline, bile ..."

Deanna fell into a state of deep concentration. I knew that she had a good knowledge of anatomy and assumed that she was giving her part a thoroughly scientific tour—and so I was quite surprised when she gave me a worried look and said, "There's a spider in there. It's racing around in my blood."

"Hmm. Well, ask your thyroid part: Does it know this spider?"

"No. It's not supposed to be there."

The spider was zipping around so quickly that neither Deanna nor her part could get a good look at it.

"Why not try stunning it a little—just enough to slow it down."

After a moment, she said, "It's a daddy longlegs."

"Ask the thyroid part what it means to have a daddy longlegs in your bloodstream."

"That's easy. Spiders are always busy."

"So it's a workaholic bug."

"Exactly. I caught it from my father."

We both laughed.

"Has this spider had an effect on the thyroid gland?" I asked.

She furrowed her brow and said that the thyroid gland was covered in a sticky gray sludge, like cobwebs.

I asked the part if it had found any other problems on its tour of the body.

"Just that spider."

"Did it check everything—the heart, liver, nervous system, pancreas, stomach, spleen? Just make sure."

She seemed to concentrate, and then said with a shudder that there were more spiders hatching inside her—a whole thicket of them was nestled in the crook of an artery. Even as we spoke, they were unfurling their legs and getting ready to swim into the bloodstream.

I took a moment to reflect. We had spiders in the bloodstream and cobwebs gumming up the thyroid gland. There was obviously little point in clearing out the cobwebs until we had dealt with the spiders. I asked the thyroid part if it knew where the spiders were originating.

"They're hatching from little eggs."

"Where are the eggs coming from?"

Deanna paused to reflect; then shook her head.

"That's okay," I said. "Just ask the part to take a closer look at those eggs. What can it sense about them?"

"Oh!" she said. "I hear Dad's voice."

"What does that sound like?"

"Like a broken record."

"What is the broken record saying?"

"All the usual imperatives. It's making the spiders zip around even faster."

"When the spiders zip faster, how does that make you feel?"

"Like I have to do, do, do."

"How would you and the part like to be free of Dad's voice?"

"We'd like that."

I asked the part to make a big stretchy container. "This container has two things about it: There's a tube that can suck like a vacuum, and you can also chuck stuff into it."

The part got to work with eager abandon. It threw out the spiders first, and then the pressure, the urgency and the blind obedience to a workaholic regime. We cleared the residue of these things out of all the body's systems. The part spontaneously volunteered to toss out its test tubes with their cautionary red lines, along with the energy plug that was limiting its production. The cobwebs went last—the part sucked them out with the vacuum, and then went to work with a scrub brush.

"How is the thyroid gland looking now?" I asked.

Deanna heaved a great sigh and slid down in her chair. Her face was pale, as usual, but her eyes gleamed. She described the thyroid gland as pink and healthy.

"There's a feeling of spaciousness to the actual physical organ. The part can see that it is the energy that lives in this space and fills it."

"How does that feel?" I asked.

"Wonderful."

She spent a moment enjoying the feeling; then sat up in her chair and said she was hungry. We decided to take a lunch break. Half an hour later, when we returned and took our seats, Deanna complained of a band of tension around the top of her head. With no prompting from me, she said, "I know what's causing this. It's a part of me that's worried about the changes we're making."

"Ask this worried part what job it does for you."

"It stops me from rushing into things that I might regret later."

"What did it regret rushing into?"

The part recalled an incident from childhood—the time Deanna and some friends had been bouncing on the family sofa and had broken the springs.

"I don't think I've ever seen Dad so angry."

"What decision did the worried part make when that happened?"

"To think very hard about all the possible results of any given action."

"Hmm. Well ask the worried part: What does it think of that healthy pink thyroid gland?"

"It can do its job. That's not a problem."

"So what exactly triggered it to start getting worried now?"

"Well — it says that coming off the medication won't be easy. We don't know what will happen — not for sure."

"Ask it: What is the worst that can happen?"

"It says the same thing that happened twenty years ago, before I went on the thyroid pills. Deanna will keep sleeping in and lose her job."

"And what will happen then?"

"She won't be able to get another job."

"And then what?"

"She'll lose her apartment."

"And then?"

Deanna grimaced. "The part knows that I would not move back in with my parents. That would be the absolute worst."

As I explained to Deanna, the role of a worrier part is to conjure up all the bad things that could possibly result from any given action. By projecting these dire consequences into the future, worry parts not only make us fearful, they make it harder to succeed when we do take action — since we tend to attract what we focus on.

I asked the part again, "So what do you think of Deanna's plan to go off her medication?"

"She has no idea what's going to happen."

"Yes she does," I countered gently. "She has an idea that her thyroid is going to kick back in and help her establish her own rhythms. In fact, she's been talking about this for several weeks now. Where have you been?"

"Um, w-well," the part stuttered, "I've been worrying."

We laughed, but I knew the part's concerns were very real to it. In an attempt to reassure it, I asked it to consider Deanna's recent history. She had worked on her allergies and they had disappeared. Furthermore, she had carefully thought through her plan to reactivate her thyroid gland, even soliciting the help of her doctor.

"Do you think that she has planned this carefully enough?"

"Yes, but—." Deanna was smoothing her skirt over her knees, as if trying to iron out every wrinkle.

"But what?" I prompted.

She looked sheepish. "The part says it will have nothing to do if it stops worrying."

"Well that's a legitimate concern," I commented. "Ask the part: What does it believe about doing and having something to do?"

"That's its whole reason for being."

"Where did it learn that?"

"From Dad."

"So the part needs something to do, but it's adopted Dad's pattern of doing and it's imposed that energy on Deanna. Is it aware that Deanna wants to restore her own patterns and rhythms?"

She chewed her lip. "It does know that. And it would like to cooperate. It feels it's been misguided more than anything."

"Yes, it has been misguided," I agreed. "And it's been bullied. But let the part know that it belongs to you, not to Dad. The days of being bullied by Dad are over."

Deanna laughed. "The part just stood up and dusted itself off. It's coming forward with an armload of objects that it wants to throw out."

"What objects?"

"They're hard and lumpy, with sharp edges."

"Are they Deanna's?"

"No—it's all Dad's stuff."

She showed the part the already brimming container and it dumped its load on top. We then made sure that it cleared out all the negatives, including Dad's imperatives and the pressure and tension that had resulted.

As these things drained out, Deanna began to relax. She slumped right down in her chair—head resting back, legs stretched out and arms dangling. The worry part, she said, had melted and become formless.

"Does it still have an identity?"

"Oh yes—that's not a problem. But it doesn't have the tension to hold a particular shape."

In fact, the part had become a pool of water—deep and clear. The water was sparkling and full of energy.

Because the part had changed form I wanted to be sure it still felt connected to Deanna. Normally, I might suggest that she give it a hug, but since it was a pool I proposed instead that she jump into it.

"It likes that."

Floating in the pool, she said, felt "warm and cushiony." There was a sensation of weightlessness, as if the water were supporting her.

"It's odd. All I want to do is lie here, and yet I feel this tremendous energy coursing through me."

I couldn't have been more pleased. To my knowledge, this was the first time Deanna had tapped into an internal energy source that was independent of food or sleep—and it was certainly going to come in handy. I asked the thyroid part if it would like to join Deanna in the pool. Jumping in with a splash, it too was bathed in the healing warmth and energy. After a while it began to change color, taking on the clear, sparkling blue of the water.

"What is the pool discovering about itself?" I asked.

"It's an energy matrix—a pool of pure energy."

"And what is the purpose of this matrix?"

"To energize. That seems to be its sole purpose."

"Ask it to take a look around. Can it tell where the energy comes from?"

She turned up her palms. "It's life force."

"Can the part sense where that originates?"

"It's always been there."

I must say, Deanna looked positively radiant. I thought that if I drew the curtains and doused the lights I might see her glowing in the dark.

"It's wonderful," she said.

I think she and her part would have been happy to stay in the pool forever. It was with some regret at disrupting their blissful sojourn that I suggested to the part that it was time to return to its home base in the throat. I needn't have worried, though. As the part emerged, the pool's energy simply expanded and went with it.

"The pool just stretched without losing any density," said Deanna with a delighted laugh.

Not one to neglect an opportunity, I asked the pool to "look around" and see if there were any other physical organs that would benefit from its energy. Without a moment's hesitation it flowed into all the organs and filled up the entire body. Deanna seemed to fall into an even deeper state of relaxation, if that was possible.

I took a moment to glance at my notes and consider what remained to be done. I had to remind myself that this amazing energy matrix was actually the former worrier part. Both it and the thyroid had undergone major transformations. My main concern now, I decided, was to make sure the thyroid could recapture the knowledge of its original functioning.

"Ask the thyroid part: Can it remember what it was like before all the pressure and worry came along?"

Deanna gave me a lazy smile as the part drifted back in time. "No worries," she said. "You just go along. Do your job. Nobody bothers you. Nobody interferes."

"Let the part get used to that."

"It's really easy to get used to."

"Did it have lots of energy?"

"Yes."

"What was its relationship to the other glands and organs?"

After a brief silence she said that the blue energy was in everything. Then, as now, the entire body was filled with life force and fueled by it.

"Ask the thyroid part: Back there in the blue energy, what function do you perform?"

"I help supply energy."

"Do Deanna's thoughts and feelings and actions draw energy?"

"Of course."

"So the part just gives Deanna energy and Deanna takes it."

"Takes what she needs and there's always enough."

"There is always enough energy," I repeated. "That's a useful belief."

"It's true," she said.

"Ask the part: Back then in the blue energy, is it worried about anything?"

Deanna raised her eyebrows. "What's to worry about?"

"I don't know—I was just checking. Because it was sure worried later on in life."

She shrugged. "That was Dad's stuff."

"So back then there was nothing to worry about. And what did the part know that allowed it to not have a care in the world?"

"There's an energy flow and it runs through all things, all life."

"Did the part trust that energy flow?"

"Absolutely."

"Did it think the energy would ever run dry?"

"Of course not."

I wanted the part to put into words this sense of a reliable energy source, to affirm its knowledge as a belief. I formulated my question carefully. "Given that there's always enough energy, because an energy flow runs through all things, and knowing that it can trust this energy, can the part say: I trust my energy because my energy is inexhaustible?"

Deanna looked dubious.

"Could it be committed to that? Because it forgot it later on."

"Yes, but that was because of other people's stuff."

"Sure. But because of other people's stuff the part forgot what it knew."

"This is true."

"So we need a new belief here."

She asked me to repeat the phrase I had suggested, and then sat for a moment mulling it over. She said at last, "The part can say, *my energy is inexhaustible*. It's quite definite about that. But there's something about the word *trust*. It's not that the concept is wrong but the word isn't encompassing enough."

I suggested that she ask her part for an appropriate word or phrase, but after a very long silence she shook her head and said that words just didn't fit. Unwilling to give up, I proposed some alternate phrases, basing them on words the part itself had used. Each time, she shook her head. At length I suggested, "I am one with life force," and she raised a hand.

"I am one with *life*," she amended.

Her hand remained poised in the air, and as she repeated the phrase tears poured from her eyes and streamed down her cheeks. I knew that she had finally found the right words.

When she had taken a moment to cry, laugh and dry her eyes, I asked her where she was feeling the energy most in her body.

She patted her stomach. "That's where it's radiating from."

"This is your own energy," I said. "You might want to add to your beliefs: *My energy belongs to me.* People sometimes forget they own themselves."

"Yes, well a lot of people try to convince them otherwise."

We finished the process by bringing the thyroid gland — now infused with life energy — forward through time. Along the way, I suggested that it dissolve the entire belief-tree that had caused it to lose its energy connection, paying special attention to the belief: *Never do anything to upset Dad.*

"Make sure that one is blown sky high."

"That was at the base of the tree," said Deanna. "The whole tree just exploded."

I leaned forward and touched her lightly on the throat and forehead, places she herself had touched earlier in the session when she was describing painful feelings. As the energy came through I wanted to make sure that it flowed to these spots.

"Everything just went blue behind my eyes," she murmured.

"Invite your entire body at every level, right down to the DNA, to accept this original model for the thyroid gland and to allow its normal functioning to be restored."

She nodded.

"Blue energy all through you?" I asked.

She nodded again.

"How is the thyroid gland doing?"

"It's doing fine. It says thank you, I have my home back now."

As we stood up to stretch our legs I asked the thyroid how it felt about gradually coming off the medication. Not only was it happy with the plan, it predicted that recovery would indeed be gradual, taking place over a month or two. And that is exactly what happened.

Deanna continued to take her thyroid pills as usual. Then, two weeks after the session she began to feel restless and jittery. She paid a visit to her doctor, who confirmed that these were symptoms of hyperthyroidism — the level of thyroid hormone in her blood had risen. The doctor reduced her medication by half.

Two weeks later, Deanna was once again feeling jittery. Another meeting with her doctor resulted in her medication again being cut in half. The dose was now so small, said the doctor, that it was hardly worth taking. Two weeks after that, baffled but pleased, she took Deanna off the pills altogether.

It is now ten years since I worked with Deanna on her thyroid part. During that time she has taken no thyroid medication and her energy has remained stable and dependable.

In a happy sequel to this story, relations between Deanna and her father have taken a turn for the better. As Deanna explains it, "The shifts in my perception altered my role in the relationship — and that caused the relationship itself to change." By her own account, she now looks forward to visits with her parents and enjoys the time she spends with them.

———————————

I was, of course, very pleased with the results of this process. Things don't always fall into place so easily, and when I ask myself what made the difference here, two things come to mind. First and foremost, Deanna's thyroid disorder was no longer serving a purpose in her life. As we saw in the previous story, it did at one time contribute to her dependence on doctors, which in turn provided certain benefits. But when she left all that behind, the disorder became a mere relict of times gone by. The second factor was Deanna's confidence in her ability to heal. She already had evidence that my approach worked for her, and she had complete faith that it could work again. In spite of all she had been through, it seemed that skepticism was not part of her nature. This was a rare and valuable asset. When our energies and intentions are not fractured by doubt, miracles are far more likely to occur.

It was no surprise that Deanna's thyroid part was in trouble, given its quid pro quo ideas about energy. According to the part, eating and sleeping provided a given amount of energy, which was then expended in a given amount of work. In this system, energy was strictly proscribed by food taken in and hours slept. Once it found the energy pool, however, the part had access to large and constant reserves.

As Deanna's story so beautifully demonstrates, it is not always necessary to stay with an anatomically correct model of the body when working with physical symptoms at the mental/emotional level. While the conscious mind holds whatever model of health it has learned or pieced together, the subconscious has its own unique perspective—primitive yet brilliant—and its own way of understanding and representing the physiology. It is essential that we honor and respect this intuitive and imaginative knowledge. We do this when we work with naturally occurring imagery.

We have moved beyond the days when it was the therapist's job to "interpret" the subjective contents of the subconscious. Words, sounds, colors and images signify different things to each of us, and so there can be no collectively meaningful lexicon of symbols. Deanna envisioned life energy as a pool of sparkling water, whereas others would see it differently. And where her spiders represented a workaholic mentality, this would not necessarily be true for the next person. Only by trusting ourselves and respecting our unique inner worlds can we find the answers we need to galvanize our innate and distinctly individual powers of healing.

Half in Love with Easeful Death

When he first came to see me in March 1987, Mark had known for just over a year that he was HIV-positive. He couldn't say for sure when he had been infected but thought it was in the late 1970s — for him, a period of partying and promiscuity in West Coast gay bars and bath houses. Now, a decade later, his immune system was in an alarming state of decline.

HIV (human immunodeficiency virus) is among the most treacherous of microorganisms because it attacks the immune system itself, killing the very cells that are meant to disarm it — and multiplying in the process. The immune-system cells most susceptible to HIV are CD4 cells — whose job is to detect the presence of invading pathogens. As the virus kills off the CD4s the immune function weakens, leaving the body increasingly susceptible to infection and disease. When serious infection develops a person is said to have AIDS (acquired immune deficiency syndrome).

At the time Mark and I joined forces doctors relied on CD4 counts to chart the progress of HIV in individuals. This test measures the number of these cells in a cubic millimeter of blood, giving an indication of how much damage the virus has done. While most healthy adults have a CD4 count of 600 to 1500, Mark's count when we began working was just 430.

CD4 counts can vary when taken at different times of day or by different labs, but the long-term trend they indicate gives a fairly reliable measure of immune-system function — or dysfunction, as the case may be. When the CD4 count falls below 200, one is considered at risk of developing any number of opportunistic infections, including PCP (pneumocystis carinii pneumonia), a leading cause of death among people with AIDS.

I took Mark on as a research case. I had no experience working with HIV and did not know what was possible. But I hoped that by resolving the psychological components of the disease we might be able to effect a cure. Mark, however, was skeptical. Of course he wanted to be cured but he found it hard to believe that it could happen outside of a medical breakthrough. His main reason for coming to me, he said, was to find some happiness while he still had the chance. I decided, therefore, that my main task would be to reduce his psychological stress as much as possible. Not only would this improve his frame of mind, but knowing that stress suppresses the immune system, I theorized that the more stress we could alleviate the better his immune function would be and the healthier he would remain. Mark agreed to this plan, though he felt that at best we could only delay the inevitable.

As we began our first session he told me that his health had been good—so far he had suffered only minor infections like eczema and athlete's foot. His emotional complaints, however, were near encyclopedic: He spoke of low self-esteem, fear of failure, perfectionism, procrastination, depression, a tendency to use food, alcohol and marijuana to dull himself—the list went on and on. Most alarming to me was that he had no dreams or plans for the future. Even before his diagnosis, he said, his future had been a blank because he had no idea what he wanted to do with his life. All his woes were magnified by the belief that he would be dead in a few years. He had watched many friends and acquaintances die painful deaths from AIDS-related illnesses, and found himself obsessing more and more on both the failures of his life and the horrors that awaited him.

I asked him which of his many concerns was weighing on him most heavily. His perfectionism and fear of intimacy, he said, were destroying his love life. His boyfriend Keith he described as temperamentally his opposite — open, affectionate and reckless — and by comparison Mark felt himself to be uptight and defensive. His eyes, behind his glasses, showed a gleam of despair.

When asked what he wanted to accomplish during the session, he said, "I'd like to be more open in my relationships — to feel more comfortable with my vulnerability."

"So let's begin by talking to the part of you that feels uptight and defensive. Ask inside if that part would be willing to speak with you in consciousness."

He closed his eyes. "It's right here," he said, placing a hand on his chest.

"Ask the part what job it does for you," I instructed.

"It says it keeps people at arm's length."

"And ask it: What is the benefit of keeping people at arm's length?"

"It wants to protect me from the pressures and impositions that go hand-in-hand with close relationships."

"Where did the part learn this about relationships?"

"From my parents."

From Mark's father, the part told us, it had learned that people will try to force you into a mold if you let them get too close. His mother, on the other hand, had done "the Christian thing" and given herself up totally to the needs of others. But in doing so she had ended up an unhappy slave, as the part had keenly observed.

"Small wonder I'm not good at intimacy," Mark commented.

"What do you consciously believe about intimacy?" I asked.

He frowned. "I'm wary of it. But I'd like to have it."

"Would you need to be so wary if you first learned to be more intimate with yourself?"

"That's an interesting thought."

"Because that's the first step here. Intimacy with self sets the pattern for how you have intimacy with others. You have tender spots, sexual spots, mean spots and mischievous spots. Intimacy is embracing all of that and saying: I'm okay with it."

"I've always had a fear that if I look too closely I'll find out that I'm really shallow."

Knowing this is never true, I suggested that if we discovered he was shallow, then the answers would be obvious and our work would be easier. We both laughed.

The uptight part felt more hopeful after this exchange and even relaxed a little, judging from a slight alleviation of Mark's visible tension. Mark was indeed a very tense individual, and yet I found him most enjoyable to work with. He was intelligent, perceptive about himself and candid in revealing what was on his mind. From my point of view, his tendency to be dry and factual was a plus—it meant that he was good at reporting what his parts had to say.

We concluded the session by taking the part to a rollover, a time in infancy when it felt open and at ease, and bringing the open feeling forward to be with Mark in the present.

A month later I called Mark to see how he was doing. He reported some improvement in his relationships—both with his family and with Keith. But I gathered that the changes were not dramatic and that he had lost enthusiasm for our work. I didn't see him for nearly two years. When he finally did appear for another session he told me that he had been more depressed than ever. His CD4 count was now down to 280. To make matters worse he and Keith, after a brief spell of harmony, had reverted to their old pattern of bickering and accusation. He did not believe that our work or anything else could help him.

I asked him what had prompted his visit, considering that he'd given up on himself. It was a practical matter, he said—a job dilemma. He was trying to make a decision and wanted to talk things over.

For some years he had held a management position with a large company, making a good salary but feeling dissatisfied. He longed to change jobs, but that would mean giving up his insurance package—and because he was HIV-positive he would not be eligible for similar insurance in a new job. What would become of him if he had no income when he finally succumbed to AIDS? As we talked the problem through he realized that he was not quite ready to make a move. For the moment, he concluded, he would bide his time and see how things developed.

But now, I decided, it was time for a change of approach. I had so far taken a laissez-faire stance with Mark—inviting him to call me if he felt like it. But I could see that his depression was getting the better of him. I encouraged him to make a commitment to our work, pointing out that even if we couldn't cure him we could certainly improve his state of mind. I also let him know that I was very concerned about his fatalistic attitude, which could not be helping his health. I, for one, chose to believe that he could survive.

"Somehow," I said, "we'll find a way to make it happen."

The consensus out there, especially in the medical profession, is that it's cruel to arouse "false" hope in the sick and dying. And yet it is well known that hope and optimism are important ingredients in healing. In my view, as long as there was the slightest chance that Mark could make it, his energy was best used to fuel that possibility.

"If you try and fail," I admonished, "you will at least know that you've done what you can."

At the same time, I said, it wasn't a bad thing that he was confronting his mortality. Coming to grips with the democratic process of death should ideally be done long before a person is actually facing it.

My pep talk must have had some effect because soon afterwards he arrived for another session. After much discussion about what to work on we decided to explore the part that had drawn the virus to him. I began with my usual inquiry.

"Ask inside if the part responsible for attracting the virus into your life will communicate with you in consciousness."

He sat sideways in his chair, legs crossed, head bent pensively forward. After a moment's silence he began to laugh.

"I have pictures of descending ladders. There's a deep pit with smoke coming out of it. The word spiritual comes to mind."

"Interesting. What does the word spiritual mean to you?"

"I'm aware of a propensity I've had for traveling inward and discovering parts of myself and my relationship to God."

In short, he explained, his infection was forcing him to wake up and take stock of his inner state, as he may not have much time left to work on it.

"How many parts are involved in this internal search?" I asked.

He gave this a moment's thought, extending his fingers as he counted. "Five altogether."

"Let's look at them one by one."

The first he called his courageous part. As we explored its history, we found it had a habit of swallowing anger when Mark didn't get what he wanted.

"Having what you want is selfish," said the part. "In order for Mark to be satisfied, somebody else has to give something up."

"What does satisfy this part?" I asked.

"Moments when I'm by myself and don't have to relate to anyone else's wishes and desires."

Next was a heart part that was also plagued by others' demands. But although the part was angry about this, it always gave in.

The third part, a sexual part, told us that its job was to suppress Mark's vitality. Where had it learned to do this? It could cite any number of incidents—for example, the time when twelve-year-old Mark had gone to confession and talked to the priest about masturbation.

"He was very harsh. I was quite stunned by his vehemence and anger."

Another part, located in the brow, kept itself totally above the fray and detached from all the other parts. This brow part was curious — it liked to read and explore. It could go on doing these things regardless of what was happening in Mark's life. I liked the fact that Mark had such a bright part, and I knew that it remained detached only because there was so much to deny.

The final part was a coordinator, which had the difficult task of keeping the other four parts working together.

"I'm the one who introduced the virus to Mark," it told us with a hint of pride.

I asked the part what its intention had been in doing that.

"Mark needed to slow down and get in touch with himself."

"So I wonder, now that Mark is making a sincere effort to do just that, has the HIV infection become redundant?"

Mark (the part) gave me a cynical smile. "Not at all. Mark is extremely lazy. In order to accomplish anything he needs a deadline, such as that imposed by impending death."

After negotiating with each of the parts, I addressed them as a group, guiding them back through time.

"Ask them to remember how it was before they made all these decisions: that you have to live up to everyone's expectations, that getting what you want is selfish, that you must suppress your vitality, that you have to remain aloof in order to hold onto a piece of yourself — and that Mark can't accomplish anything unless he is threatened with a deadline."

Drifting deeper and deeper into Mark's past, the parts finally came to a place where they were "joined together as a single entity."

"What is that like?" I asked Mark.

"I see a core of light. The parts are sheets of lightning—like electric leaves—coming out from the core."

"How does it feel?"

"It feels magical."

"Ask this core of light that encompasses all the parts: Can it remember where its magic comes from?"

"It always was and will always be."

Mark's eyes gleamed softly. I felt very moved and very much in tune with his exhilaration.

"Who are you?" I asked the part.

"Light and love."

"Does this part know who Mark is?"

"I am Mark," the part replied simply.

We brought the core of light forward through time, activating it in Mark's present-day life. When I was satisfied that he was feeling its effects I ventured to ask if it was within this part's power to heal the HIV infection.

"Not without Mark's support," said the part—and Mark admitted that he felt skeptical. "Or maybe I should say that my skeptic has arrived on the scene."

I received this news with a quickening of resolve. I knew that Mark's skeptic part had been influencing him and felt much happier dealing with it head on than having it sabotage our work from the sidelines. Besides, Mark needed to get better acquainted with this rather cynical aspect of his personality. With such a prominent part of him doubting that he could be cured, we were pitted against strong odds indeed. Not that belief alone is always enough to cure an illness—but when there is no belief in even the possibility of healing, there is no energy being channeled in that direction.

I asked the skeptic if it would be willing to support and strengthen the work we had just done.

"Is that a skeptic's role?" the part countered.

"What is your role as a skeptic?" I asked.

"To ensure that Mark is pragmatic, realistic, and doesn't go off on some half-cocked course only to be disappointed later."

It was no surprise to learn that the skeptic had disappointment on its mind. What many skeptics fear most is being let down.

"How often have you been disappointed?" I asked it.

"Too many times to count."

"Are you most disappointed by other people or do you tend to disappoint yourself?"

"More often than not I disappoint myself."

"How?"

"By having really high expectations of myself and trying to be perfect."

I asked the part whose standards it was trying to live up to. Mark's gaze drifted along the floor as he searched for the answer. "Mom's," he said finally.

"Are any of those standards your own?"

"Not till I adopted them."

"I'd like you to take a look at that consciously, Mark: I'm disappointed in myself based on Mom's idea of what I should be doing."

The skeptic had not only stored Mom's high standards, it was also carrying Dad's disappointment in himself. And yet, while willing to acknowledge that none of this belonged to Mark, the part maintained that what Mark and I were doing could not be called "healing" with any degree of certainty.

"What can it be called?" I asked.

"Integration," the part replied. Mark looked at me thoughtfully. "Which is interesting," he said, "because I do know that the disintegration of parts can result in physical chaos."

"Aha," I said. "Does that mean that if parts integrate mentally and emotionally it can produce the opposite of physical chaos?"

"That seems reasonable."

"So ask the part: What is the opposite of physical chaos?"

"The word that comes to mind is healing," he acknowledged. We both laughed at this turnaround.

From here I went a step further, commenting that any skeptic who just wanted to throw sand on the fire was not a true skeptic.

"The honest skeptic is willing to learn," I said. "Many people call themselves skeptics yet all they do is blindly invalidate. Those are the people who try to convince you that you can't heal yourself. The cause-and-effect world of medicine and Newtonian science have had so much influence on our beliefs that most people can't conceive of going outside those parameters."

I asked the part how it went about its skepticism.

"I doubt. I ask myself if I'm deluding myself in some way."

"Do you decide when it's appropriate to doubt? Or do you just doubt everything on principal?"

"I doubt everything."

"Does blindly doubting allow you to make discernments?"

Mark shook his head. "Of course not."

I asked the part, "Can you see that something in Mark is being integrated or healed through our work today?"

"Tentatively, yes."

"What do you think the result of this could be?"

"I guess we'll find out."

"Are you in favor of Mark healing or not?"

"In favor."

"When you constantly question whether you're deluding yourself, does that lend energy to healing or disintegration?"

"Disintegration."

"So we know those thoughts are not useful. But the part has to have thoughts. Skeptics are thinking parts. The problem is, it's equated skepticism with doubt, and although it knows that doubt takes away from healing it's afraid that if we believe in healing everything will come crashing down and we'll be terribly disappointed."

As Mark looked at me I could see the skeptic in him warily assessing these ideas. I plunged ahead, taking a new tack.

"Ask the part if it only looks for flaws. Does it also look for successes?"

"No. It looks for flaws."

"Can it think about the possibility of finding flaws in its own strategy?"

"Yes."

"Ask it: Is there a flaw in what it's been doing?"

"The flaw is that it's destructive—it's grating and nagging and undermines my belief in myself. I'm defeated before I even start."

Pleased that the part was so quick to learn, I moved the questioning in another direction.

"What is the benefit of undermining your belief in yourself?"

Looking at his hands Mark said, "That way, I don't have to do anything—like be responsible for myself or take control of my life."

"Ask the part to think back. When did it decide that it didn't want to have to do things?"

"Mark's been trying all his life and deserves a break."

"Is it time for a break?"

"Yes." Mark ran a hand through his hair. "It's this business of always having to fight parts inside myself that are going off in different directions—and then always aspiring to fulfill other people's expectations. One of the benefits of HIV is that I won't have to try anymore because I'll be dead."

He told me a story.

"When I was in grade twelve I had an algebra test coming up and didn't want to take it because I knew I'd fail. The morning of the test I had an appendicitis attack and was rushed to the hospital. As I was lying in the ambulance I was in such excruciating pain that I left my body. Once outside my body and looking down at myself I felt relaxed and calm.

"I remember going back in and again feeling pain, but while I was waiting in line for emergency surgery the pain disappeared and they sent me home."

He paused, giving me a weary smile. I smiled back. This was not the first time I'd come across a part that could mimic physical symptoms.

"So I got out of taking the test," said Mark. "And I also understood that death is a release — that whatever pressures I built up in myself could be released through death."

"Do you and the part think it's easier to die than measure up to certain standards?"

"In a way, yes. I've given so much of myself to other people's expectations, it feels like there's nothing left."

"So death is a release. Does that mean you would object to healing yourself?"

"No."

"But it seems you'll do anything to avoid failure. Have you ever played with the concept that there is no such thing as failure? That everything is a learning experience?"

"I've heard that said. And it's a more useful construction than the earlier one — where stubborn habitual behavior has led to the same mistakes over and over."

"So everything is a learning experience, including learning to heal yourself. This part may even know how to do that, considering that it healed you instantly from appendicitis."

Mark laughed.

"How old does the part think you are?"

"It says three."

"So it's been guarding you as if you were a three-year-old — as if you were blindly gullible, with no ability to discern."

"Yes, it's been disrespectful."

"Did the part hear that?"

He suddenly grinned. "It can grudgingly accept that I'm forty."

"Ask the skeptic to look at that brow part that we talked to earlier. Has it ever been able to keep Mark's mind as sharp as that?"

"No. It hasn't been discerning."

"What about the core of light? How does it view this skeptic and the doubts that it's raised?"

Mark closed his eyes. "The skeptic is just a minuscule part, very far away. It's dust."

"Would the skeptic like to sense and feel what Mark has tapped into with this core of light?"

"Yes."

"Ask it to go back in its memory. What was it doing before it adopted Mom's standards and before it felt disappointed?"

"It was part of the light."

"And when it was part of the light, what were its hopes and dreams?"

"To live happily, energetically, enthusiastically."

"Looking forward from there, what does it see?"

"As we go forward I see it splitting off. That happened in the womb."

"What caused it to split off in the womb?"

"Mom wasn't sure she wanted me."

"And what did it split off from? What got left behind?"

"Enthusiasm."

"Consciously, Mark, would you be willing to re-embrace that enthusiasm?"

"Of course."

"Ask the part to go back before that huge disappointment when it got the feeling that it wasn't wanted. How did it feel before it turned the enthusiasm off?"

"Great."

"Can it feel, in that enthusiasm, what it's like to be part of the light?"

"Yes."

"Ask it to bring that energy forward and literally dissolve all separations that have been caused by the denial of its enthusiasm."

As the part projected itself through time we made sure it unloaded the expectations of others that it had been storing and the belief that *death is the only way out*. It also dissolved the belief, *I'm not wanted*, replacing it with its own conviction, *I want me*.

I found it fascinating that the skeptic part had turned out to be a splinter. So often, we do fragment ourselves in this way, leaving behind bits of ourselves that we believe to be inappropriate or unacceptable.

With the integration of Mark's skeptic into the core of light the process was complete. But I knew from experience that doubting, like worrying, can become an ingrained habit, especially if the conscious mind is participating, as Mark's had been. It is the job of consciousness to think past old assumptions and limitations. Parts instinctively support no change until consciousness leads the way.

I said to Mark, "If those doubting thoughts should recur, realize that you don't have to buy into them. It's important that you participate with your part in learning how to discern rather than doubt."

After this session, which took place early in 1989, Mark seemed to become much more grounded in his quest for healing and survival. To me, this indicated that his skepticism had transformed to a significant degree. He made a commitment to our work and appeared for sessions more frequently. On top of this he took my advanced training course, in which he gave and received numerous processes (none of which are documented). He occasionally tried other healing methodologies but was not drawn to working with anyone else on an ongoing basis. His CD4 count was holding steady and the only sign of a depressed immune system was a fungal spot on his tongue.

Over the next two years Mark and I got together about once every four months. This was plenty considering the depths we plumbed on each occasion. It wasn't long before he reported a decided improvement in his outlook. He also began taking better care of himself: exercising more, keeping regular hours and practicing daily meditation. The only problem was that his CD4 count again began to plummet. As 1990 came to a close it fell to 170, and he found himself plagued by thrush and yeast infections.

"I'm tired of fighting," he said.

Now, at last, he decided to follow his doctor's advice and go on AZT, an anti-HIV drug then in common use. For him, as for so many others, the dangers posed by potential side-effects lost significance when stacked against the alternative: illness, debilitation and death. With the goal of alleviating both his apprehension and his susceptibility to side-effects, we spent a session working with his fear of drugs.

As we continued to forge ahead, I found that as soon as one thing got resolved Mark would immediately identify another issue that was tormenting him. In early 1991 his concerns centered around his relationship with Keith. Their sex life was dead, he complained, and they no longer had any fun. He felt bottled up and unable to express his feelings.

I noticed that Mark's parts tended to come in pairs. In one instance we worked with an expressive part that went into retreat at the signal of a shy part. The shy part wanted to hide Mark's life force from what it perceived as the neediness of his mother. While Mark himself had always loved his mother, this part saw her as a vampire who sucked his energy. As we worked with the shy part it came across a brilliant diamond that it had stashed away where Mother couldn't find it.

"The diamond is my life," said the part.

Indeed, Mark was continually finding bits and pieces of himself hidden in boxes or lodged behind walls—fragments that were asleep or tucked away for safekeeping. As a boy he had got the impression that he was no good and so had closed himself off in different ways, yet everything we found in these closed-off areas was filled with light and value. There was a hoard of fresh fruits and vegetables, a chest of jewels and a stash of "fine qualities and good intentions." Each time we came across such a treasure we integrated it and ran its energy through his system to see what healing value it might have.

We did find one or two links between sex and death, but these turned out to be superficial. More significant were the links between sex and guilt or sex and punishment. Mark had an incredibly complex mind and the strategies his parts had created over the years kept us both on our toes.

As 1991 progressed he began to feel that real change was taking place within him. He finally found the strength to quit his job, and not long after that he and Keith decided to separate. Yet, even as he was telling me that he loved himself more, he continued to complain that life was tedious and exasperating.

"There's so little return—and there's no promise for the future. Only in death can there be relaxation."

In one session we worked with what he called his compulsive eating part. He complained that he couldn't resist a daily round of pastries, even though he was trying to cut down on sugar and wheat (which his doctor related to his yeast infections). The eating part accused Mark outright of being stingy and uptight.

"You'll die sooner if you don't allow yourself these small plea-sures," the part scolded.

Exuberant, intense and hedonistic, the eating part wanted Mark to lighten up and have more fun. Its energy was clearly valuable and so, rather than trying to tone it down, we decided that it needed to expand its options. The part conceded that it was not always considerate—for instance when it stuffed Mark so full of goodies that he felt sick—and agreed to be more creative in its pleasure seeking. We completed the process by bringing its exuberant energy into Mark's physical body and chakras.

By the spring of 1992 Mark's CD4 count was hovering around 100 (it was 70 according to one test and 110 according to another). Because he was showing signs of liver damage his doctor took him off AZT and started him on an alternate anti-HIV medication, along with a number of other drugs designed to prevent infections. He continued to feel healthy and energetic—but his test results were disastrous to his morale. According to all he'd seen and read he had little chance of survival with a CD4 count below 100.

When he came to a session in June he presented a litany of complaints.

"I assume at the outset that I'm going to fail—that I'm just not good enough—that people will find a reason not to like me. I'm unable to make decisions. I'm afraid for my health and my financial security. I feel sad, angry and disappointed in myself. Sometimes I don't even know what I'm feeling. I'm running out of hope."

I asked him what he wanted to work on. He felt that he needed to face life with a more flexible, free-flowing attitude.

"I want to be able to recognize my internal messages and trust myself sufficiently to execute them."

We conversed with a part that he called his creative director, which appeared in his mind as a tense young man hunched over a control panel. The part's job was to generate and attract possibilities, which was fine except that it invited things willy-nilly into Mark's life. Created when Mark was a boy, the part's original purpose had been to provide relief from a dreary life.

"But it's turned into a chaos generator," said Mark.

I wondered if this creative director had anything to do with attracting Mark's HIV infection. Although we had already worked with a disease part that claimed to have drawn the virus into

Mark's life, I knew that a serious disease usually answers the needs of many parts.

I asked the creative director: "Among all the possibilities you have attracted, was HIV one of them?"

"That was a clever one, wasn't it?" the part quipped.

"Was that one of your ideas for escaping from a dreary life?"

"Certainly."

I looked at Mark speculatively. "I'd like you to ask this part: Is life not getting kind of dreary with the worry and anguish that's been generated through the HIV?"

He shrugged. "What would you suggest?"

"My suggestion is almost irrelevant. Because every ingredient that's needed to heal Mark is inside of Mark."

"This part doesn't see that it has the depth or capacity to heal me."

"Yet it has the capacity to create illness."

Mark (the part) laughed. "You flatter me my dear."

"We're simply asking the part to think about maturing in what it's doing."

Still, the part did not feel able. It agreed that it would like to slow down and be more discriminating about what it attracted, but maintained that it was much easier to get HIV than to get rid of it.

"The part feels it would have to search far and wide to find a cure. And how could it possibly succeed where so many research scientists have failed?"

I was wondering where to go from here when Mark offered an observation. "As a creative director the part is mainly interested in good stories."

My own creative director jumped in. "What about the story of a man who searched the world for a cure, and one day found that the answer was within himself. And that the answer went so deep that he spent the rest of his life exploring it — but in the process his physical condition began to improve until it was back again to what we would call good health."

I waited, curious to see if Mark would engage with me in my improvisation. To my relief, he asked, "Is it important that he believe in the possibility of that kind of an outcome in order to generate the story?"

"Did he believe in the possibility of the negative outcome?"

He hesitated. "It doesn't matter. He's kind of amoral."

"Well, I would say that him believing it is part of the equation."

"That's the germ of an interesting story."

I added that I was reminded of a statement made by the American hypnotherapist Milton Erikson: "I continue to pretend to help people and they continue to pretend to be helped, and their life gets better and better."

"Of course, anything is possible in the context of a story," said Mark.

"Would it make a difference if the part made a commitment to any one story?" I asked.

"Sure it would make a difference. In order to focus on one thing he would have to change his ways. And he would like that. He's tired of the randomness. He would like to slow down and focus on quality rather than quantity."

"Fair enough," I said. "So let's give him something to think about. There are two things Mark really wants right now: to heal himself and to have a reason for being alive as far as his work in the world is concerned. Could the part weave a story that would answer those needs?"

Like the creative director he was, the part was delighted with this challenge, and I turned my attention to another concern. I guessed that the part could still be harboring much of the dreariness of Mark's childhood experience, for which his generation of random possibilities had become the antidote. But when I asked Mark how much of the old dreariness was still weighing the part down, he looked at me blankly.

"Has the part got that stored somewhere?" I persisted.

"I don't think so. He's simply become dreary in his methodical repetition of generating possibilities."

"Hmm. Well just ask him to look at the environment around his work station."

The part's work station, Mark explained, was lit up by the monitors he was operating, but the rest of the room was dark.

"Ask the part to turn and face the darkness."

Mark closed his eyes.

"What does this darkness mean to him?"

"The part makes pictures so that it doesn't matter what happens out there. As long as he has this internal life he's okay."

"Ask him to examine this darkness that surrounds him. How thick is it?"

"Four or five feet. Sufficiently thick that it doesn't let light in."

"Can he put some probes into it and tell us what thoughts or beliefs are out there?"

Mark took off his glasses, rubbed them against his shirt and put them on again, as if to see better in the dark room. He recited the part's beliefs one by one, pausing after each. "*Life is dull … there's no future … there's no point in trying … this is all pretty boring … life is kind of sticky.*"

"What makes life sticky?"

"This black stuff."

"What is the main feeling in that stuff?"

"Partly anger, partly sadness. It's also very draining. It sucks life."

Mark said that it was the life-sucking quality of the blackness that forced the part to continually generate pictures and ideas. He added that the part did not like me for making him look at this.

"I can understand that. But ask him if any of that life-sucking energy belongs to Mark."

"No."

"Where does it come from?"

"Some is Mom's, some is Dad's, some comes from society in general."

"Would the part like his environment to be free of this?"

"Yes."

I asked Mark to join the creative director at his work station.

"Help him create a trough out here in the consultation room, and ask him to start draining out the black stuff and all the feelings and thoughts within it."

When the blackness had been emptied into the trough, Mark reported that the part had become a small baby, asleep in his arms.

"Let him know that you finally figured out how to come back for him."

"He's smiling."

"Ask him to go back in his memory to a time before he knew anything about dreariness."

Mark studied his knees. After a while he began to speak very quietly. "There's a long tunnel going back—it's miles and miles long. Sometimes it's pink and sometimes it's just a dark passageway. It becomes fainter and fainter till it vanishes." He paused. "Now there are all these stars."

"In that starriness, do we still feel me? Are we still an identity, a consciousness?"

"Yes."

"Where does this energy that is me come from?"

"Out there." He swept his arm in a wide gesture.

"What is out there beyond the field of stars?"

"It looks like light."

"What does the light feel like?"

"It's warm. It's white. It shimmers."

"Keep exploring. Is there any shape to it?"

"It's all around."

"Does it still feel like me?"

"Yes. But it feels like part of something else, too. In the sense that I'm not the only existence in this light."

"Within the light, what does the part know?"

"That we're all connected on this level."

"Let the part enjoy this warmth and connectedness — and allow yourself to feel it throughout your body."

He sunk down in his seat, his body and features softening perceptibly.

I continued, "Ask the part within the light: What belief do you hold about life in the physical body?"

"It's a curious manifestation. It offers all kinds of possibilities that don't exist where the part is now."

"Is there any program for disease in the light?"

"No."

"Within this light, what do you know that makes disease non-existent."

"I am whole."

"Ask the part to look forward in time, through the tunnel and into the life. Is there any program for disease there?"

"Yes, there's a tint."

"Where is the tint coming from?"

"It seems to be coming from my mother."

"Ask the part to look at the tint. What is the thought or belief that's creating it?"

He gave a small sigh as he came up with the answer. "You'll always be disappointed. You won't get what you want out of life."

"Ah. The beginning of the dreariness," I remarked. "Ask the part to check for any other beliefs that would predispose Mark to disease."

After a pause, he shook his head. "None."

"Is it possible to use the light to erase that tint?"

"Yes, I just have to turn up the intensity."

He allowed the light to stream back through the tunnel and into his life, transforming not only the tint but the remains of the dreariness and all the constrictions. The light came all the way to the present to be with Mark in his day-to-day existence.

With the process complete I did what I call an environmental verification, calling for any parts that objected to the changes Mark had made. Our old friend the skeptic made an appearance, letting us know that he had been keeping an eye on the proceedings.

"This part makes me nervous," said Mark, "but he's not as treacherous as he once was."

Mark was right. I found the skeptic greatly softened since our last contact with him. He wanted Mark to be healed and had even felt the effects of the light. I reminded this part that we were not asking him to blindly believe in anything or anybody—other than Mark himself.

"He can be skeptical about other things—but when it comes to Mark and Mark's well being, we do want his complete trust and support."

The skeptic found this request reasonable and agreed.

As the session thus ended I felt thankful that Mark had been able to reach such a profound level within himself. Consciously, he did not doubt his connection to a greater whole, and so his skeptical tendencies were at least not interfering on that front.

A year and a half went by before we met again. We got together just to talk, and I was pleased to learn that Mark's cell count had been holding steady at just under 100 and that he continued in good health. He told me that he was an anomaly in his community—the only other person who was still alive with a CD4 count as low as his was in "pretty bad shape." To his doctor he was a curiosity. To his friends he offered hope because he had survived and even flourished when the odds said that he should be sick. All the same, he persisted in his "realistic" outlook.

"It's inevitable that it will catch up with me. I don't plan a long-term future."

But he also acknowledged feeling more in touch with himself.

"I know now when I'm mad. And I know when I'm happy and content."

As he described it, he was more relaxed and at the same time more focused. He liked himself better and felt more a whole person, no longer torn apart by conflicting impulses. Quitting his job had helped — he was using the time to pursue his interests and meanwhile earning some money doing consulting work.

For some time I had been wanting to try working directly with Mark's HIV infection at the cellular level. Now that he was feeling basically okay with himself, the moment seemed ripe. He expressed a keen interest in the experiment, and we booked an appointment for the following week.

My plan was to explore the immune-system cells from a mental/emotional perspective. I wanted to find out what condition they were in — and help them develop a way to guard against the virus. I had never tried anything like this before and didn't know if it could work. But I did know that the body is capable of learning and adapting in more ways than we give it credit for.

We began by calling on an observer part that agreed to examine the condition of the cells and report back to us. I was not looking for scientifically accurate information — as with all parts I expected the observer to report subjectively in its own metaphorical language, which it did. On inspecting (or envisioning) a group of CD4 cells, it described them this way:

"They're steeped in some reddish-black stuff — it's like they're swimming in mud. The mud is warm and as it gets warmer the cells get more lethargic."

"What is heating up the mud?"

"Anger — I'm angry at myself for not being more and doing more."

Mark explained: "While I was still in my twenties I exceeded all my expectations and then got bored. There were no more goals to achieve because I had achieved them all—I had a good job, a fat salary and all the perks that went with that. Now I realize there's still something more I'd like to do but I don't know what it is. There's a self-rage about that."

I asked the observer to tell us what belief or thought was holding the mud in place.

"I'm not worth it," the part reported.

"That sounds like a lethargy belief," I said. "How many parts are holding that belief?"

"Lots. The belief goes way back."

"How did it come into being?"

"I see a long narrow tunnel that ends in black."

"What is in the blackness?"

"It's dark, cool, quiet."

"Ask the parts that extend back to this point: Are you still alive in that blackness?"

"Yes! We're inside Mom!" He turned faintly pink. "The 'I'm not worth it' is coming from her."

I suggested that he help the parts release the unworthy feeling since it wasn't theirs in the first place. As they did this the mud went with it. Now the observer could see the cells more clearly.

"There are both healthy cells and cells that are infected by HIV."

"Take a look at one of the infected cells."

"I see a large white cell tinged with red. Tiny things are drilling through its surface. There's a protracted struggle going on inside the cell. The virus is entwining itself in the cell's mechanism, boa-constrictor-like, becoming part of it and slowly suffocating it. I can hear a thrashing sound."

As he described this scene, he stared with evident fascination into the empty space in front of him, as if watching a movie.

"This is part of an ongoing, low-grade struggle," he added.

The healthy cells, on the other hand, were "firm, egg-shaped vessels" lacking the red tinge of the infected cells.

"There's a warm, comfortable glow to the healthy cells. As you get closer they become transparent. There's some machinery in primary colors inside."

We got into quite a technical discussion as the observer part detailed the density, humidity, electrical activity and genetic structure of both the healthy and the infected cells. The part was taking readings from an internal "control panel" that was remarkably similar to the one Deanna's health part had used (in "What the Doctor Didn't Know (I)"). With the help of this control panel the observer determined that the cells could detect a virus before it attacked. Also that each cell had the ability to "zap" a virus, using a "wavelength with a blue tint." The zapping destroyed the virus, but took so much energy that the cell was left vulnerable to further attack. Our solution was to teach the healthy cells to rally around the weakened cell and help it recover. Before the session ended we made sure all the cells were thoroughly versed in this technique.

When I heard from Mark some months later, he reported that he had been sleeping deeply and heavily ever since the session—so much so that he was getting worried about it. Knowing that cellular repair takes place during sleep, I was quite excited by this news. I advised him to relax and go with it.

Unfortunately, whatever repair might have been going on did not end up improving Mark's CD4 count. It had logged in at 70 just prior to the session and remained steady across the following months. I confess that I was disappointed. It later occurred to both Mark and I that we had overlooked the fact that HIV tends to mutate, and so had not prepared the cells for that eventuality. But of course we don't know if that would have made a difference.

A year after our cell work Mark came down with bronchitis and his CD4 count dipped to an all-time low of 20. But surprisingly, he recovered quickly, and within six months had regained some twenty cells. When we met again—this time for an informal chat—it was mid 1995, and despite his supposedly feeble immune system he continued to feel remarkably well, both mentally and physically. He had even started a new job—one with good pay that also allowed him some independence. Although he continued to be resigned to an imminent death from AIDS, he remarked that his fear and anxiety levels were way down.

"I don't know that I'd recognize the person I was ten years ago. My fundamental attitudes have changed dramatically."

In 1996 a new "cocktail" approach to AIDS treatment was introduced and proved remarkably effective. The innovation involved taking several anti-HIV drugs in combination, making it harder for the virus to mutate into drug-resistant strains. For countless AIDS patients this treatment virtually wiped out the virus and restored CD4 counts to safer levels. Many were brought back from the brink of death.

In July 1996 Mark started on this treatment with a combination of three drugs: Niveripine, Crixivan and 3TC. Within four months his CD4 count rose from 40 to 350. Other tests (measuring immune function and viral load) also indicated improvement. We were both ecstatic—and grateful that he was still alive to benefit from this medical breakthrough. As for so many others, the treatment granted him the future life that he had long despaired of. I was overwhelmed with emotion the day I attended a huge bash for his fiftieth birthday—an event that he had never expected to celebrate.

Today, Mark continues in fine health and spirits. Ongoing tests continue to show good results. Nor is he having any significant side-effects from his medication. In an e-mail he sent me some years after our final session he wrote, "I believe the work we did on my attitude towards pharmaceuticals had a very beneficial impact on my tolerance of the many drugs I've been exposed to during this long journey."

Mark told me recently that it's been years since he's spent any "mental time" on his illness. He is confident about staying alive and productive, and even remarked laughingly that he is feeling "somewhat immortal." His biggest worry, he says, is saving enough money for retirement.

A small percentage of people show strong resistance to HIV, maintaining a normal CD4 count and corresponding good health for a decade or more after becoming infected. What happened to Mark, however, is even more unusual: His immune system appeared to weaken, and yet he did not get sick. From the time of his diagnosis in 1985 until he started on the cocktail in 1996 he was seriously ill only twice: with flu in 1989 and with bronchitis in 1995. This, in spite of a CD4 count that fell below 100 in 1992 and remained there for four years. During two and a half of those years his test results fluctuated between 20 and 50, a period when he reported feeling "better and better."

How much our sessions contributed to Mark's well being and survival I can't say for sure. Yet I do know that stress can make us ill—and that over the years, as Mark and I worked together, he gradually relaxed. Not only did his inner stresses and strains dissipate, so also did his fear and anxiety about his condition. It is clear to me that even when death seems inevitable we can sometimes shift the balance—by clarifying and purifying our intent, by changing our beliefs, by removing unnecessary stress and by increasing the value of ourselves to ourselves.

Conversations with a Vagina

For a woman with a mild case of vaginismus, sexual intercourse can be painful. Lori's case was more severe. With every attempt at penetration her vaginal wall went into violent spasm. The contraction was so acute that there was no possibility of pushing past it. She simple could not have sex.

Her problem came to light in her mid-teens, during her first sexual encounter. With the thrust of a finger into her vagina, she leapt out of her boyfriend's arms in pain and alarm. The experience brought her sexual experimentation to an abrupt halt until several years later, when she fell in love. This time the result was no better, but she and Hugh decided to marry anyway, hoping that things would improve with time and patience. Unfortunately, that didn't happen. As time went on and Lori became more familiar with her body and its responses, she found that even gentle probing with her own finger caused extreme pain.

"It isn't just a case of preventing entry," she told me. "My vagina will actually expel anything that tries to get in there."

When I first met Lori she had been married to Hugh for ten years. They had given up on intercourse soon after their marriage, contenting themselves with other forms of sexual engagement. But over the years this too had come to an end and they'd settled into a pattern that involved little touching of any kind.

Meanwhile, Lori had grown discouraged. She had tried the only therapy she could find that was offered for her condition. Given a set of cylinders of gradually increasing size, she was instructed to practice inserting them into her vagina, beginning with the smallest. She made some progress over time, but when she was ready to try the real thing Hugh would not cooperate, blaming his lack of interest on stress.

"Even if it had worked," she told me, "it wouldn't have cured my indifference towards sex."

I'd had good results with other psychophysical complaints and thought Lori's condition would be simple to resolve. I can still hear myself thinking that this would be a straightforward case — one or two sessions, three at the most, and we'd be done. My optimism was perhaps fueled by Lori's impressive resolve.

"I'm sick of this," she said. "It's going to end."

I was also impressed by her warmth and openness. As we sat down for our first session in August of 1987 I remarked to myself that her appearance was unexpected, defying every conceivable stereotype of frigidity. Her lovely curves, soft brown eyes and full mouth bespoke a deeply sensual nature. Reading my thoughts, she said, "I know — when I tell people I have this problem they don't believe me."

I gave her the usual brief description of my approach, explaining that I would be asking her questions and wanted her to report whatever response came to mind, without correcting or revising it in any way.

"I'm going to start with the painful sensation around sex," I said. "There's a part of you that makes sex painful and I want you to remember that feeling."

"It stays the same, too. That feeling hasn't changed over the years."

"Is it there right now?"

"Yes."

"Can you describe it?"

It was purely physical, she explained. Her pelvis tensed up and tears came to her eyes — but there was no accompanying emotion.

"I'd like you to ask inside—just as if you were talking to yourself—if the part of you that's feeling this way would be willing to communicate."

"Yes."

"How did that answer come to you?"

"It was a really quiet voice. It came from out here." She gestured with her right hand.

"Where, specifically, is it located?"

"I feel it just behind my head."

I made a mental note that although the part had been creating tension in her pelvis it was now answering from outside her body. I asked her what the part looked like.

"It's a white form with no arms," she said.

The part showed her where it lived—in a white room with nothing in it. It liked the white room because it felt safe there.

"Safe from what?" I asked.

"From people who try to take away Lori's freedom."

"How do they do that?"

"I have an impression of somebody hugging me. It's painful."

"What does this impression mean to you?"

"I don't know. But it feels real. This person is much bigger than me. I think it's a man."

"What is the part feeling?"

"Scared."

"Can the part sense what the man is feeling?"

"There's no affection."

"If not affection, then what?"

"Spite. Lori is nothing to him." She was crying and brushed away the hair that clung to her wet cheek.

"Does the part know who the man is?"

"Oh!" she said, surprised. "It's a relative. Not my father."

"What decision did the part make when this happened?"

"I can't be hugged."

"For all time?"

"Not by somebody who doesn't understand or listen."

"Does this part know anybody who understands or listens?"

"No."

"Interesting," I said. "So we have a categorical decision that I can't be hugged because nobody understands or listens. Does that ring a bell consciously?"

"Yes. Hugging is something I've just recently learned to do."

"So you've learned it—and do you enjoy it?"

"To a point. If I can control the hug then it's okay, but if I can't get out of it then I'm uncomfortable." She took a Kleenex from a box on a sidetable and blotted her tears.

"Well, tell the part thank you for the information," I said. "What I'd like you to do is picture yourself, as you are today, walking towards the white room where the part lives. Now ask it: May I come into this room?"

"It says yes."

"Good. Picture yourself going into the room. And tell this white form: I am Lori. I'm thirty-three years old and I live in Arizona and this is who I am now. I thought you'd like to know who you are part of."

"It's surprised."

"Let it get used to the facts. Give it time. And tell it: I love you and I don't want to be separated from you anymore."

I asked Lori to explain to the part that by manifesting tension in her sexual response it was limiting her freedom. After a silence, she said, "I've told the part that I want to choose how I make love and with whom. I want the freedom to do that."

"How does the part respond?"

She compressed her lips. "It says it doesn't agree."

"In what way?"

"It says there's no freedom with sex."

"How did it learn that?"

"From Mother."

"Ah. How old were you then?"

"Six."

"And how did Mother teach you that?"

"By how she lived and what she felt."

"What did she feel about sex?"

"Fear."

"Fear of what?"

Lori looked puzzled. "Possession?" She shook herself. "This is weird. I don't remember anything about this."

I reassured her: "Sometimes the way parts perceive things is different from how we remember them consciously. I'd like you to ask the part how much of this fear is your own and how much belongs to Mother."

"Some is Lori's."

"How much is that 'some' compared to what is Mother's?"

"Most of it seems to be Mother's." She shrugged. "Mom knew more than me — she had more experience."

"Ask the part: Do you agree that Mom's fear is valid?"

She blinked. "The part has never thought to question it."

"Would the part be prepared to question it now?"

She frowned. "It wants to know why."

"Well, ask it: Whose feelings are more valid — Mother's or Lori's?"

"Protecting Lori is what matters."

"So does that make Mom or Lori more important?"

"The protection is for Lori."

"Consciously, Lori — do you agree that you need to be protected?"

Lori looked at me blankly; then put a hand to her forehead and complained of feeling dizzy.

We took a short break and I coached her through some slow deep breathing. When she had recovered her equilibrium I asked the part if it knew the difference between Mom's feelings and

Lori's feelings.

"The part is really confused," said Lori.

"Explain to this part that we have a conflict here between what it wants and what Lori wants."

"It has a hard time understanding."

"Well, it is going to be pretty hard as long as it's got Mother's fear in it. Ask the part what else it learned from Mother."

"Feelings should never be shown."

"What feelings does it have within itself that it hasn't shown?"

"It feels alone. It feels unhappy. But it doesn't mind because that's the price of being able to protect Lori."

We went around this circle several times. Alone in its empty white room, filled with the fear it had absorbed from Mother, the part had usurped a large piece of Lori's consciousness—and was now causing her earlier resolve to crumble. Yet the part did have Lori's best interests at heart. When I asked if it was protecting only itself or Lori as a whole it answered, "The whole is worth more."

"Tell the part that the whole of Lori needs to survive and grow, not just one part taking all the control."

"It can see that."

"Ask it to feel around inside itself. Can it find the energy that's just Lori?"

After a while she said, "Lori's energy feels better than the other stuff. It's warm."

"Would it rather feel that?"

"Yes."

I was pleased and touched that the part had discovered this hidden warmth within itself. Burrowing into the warmth made it feel safe and happy, and so it was finally able to let go of Mother's fearful energy.

Now that the part was not so fearful, I asked if it could remember a time before it lived in the white room. Lori closed her eyes, and then gave me a rueful look.

"It's found another white room. There's a whole row of white rooms, all connected by black strips."

The part reported that each room represented a life, an incarnation, with the stretches of blackness between the rooms signifying the periods of death between lives. According to the part, its history had been just this — a long succession of lives spent in white rooms. It had been with Lori through many lifetimes, it told us — but always hidden away in these ghostly rooms.

When I tried to discover what had made the part want to hide in the first place, it came up with a series of disjointed images that Lori associated with past lives — peering out through bars, watching a rape take place, holding the hand of a dying boy. I did my best to heal the painful feelings around these images, moving gradually toward my goal — to persuade the part to come inside the body. In the end, we used the deep pocket of warmth that the part had found hidden within itself. It expanded the warmth to fill Lori's entire body, thus making the physical a place that felt safe and inviting.

With this significant part of Lori integrated, I dared to hope for a shift in the vaginismus. But when she returned for another session a month later her feedback was mixed. She had been feeling more warmth in general, and this had led her to approach her husband for sex. This time, he'd been happy to oblige but the result was far from satisfying. Not only was penetration still impossible — the encounter had brought on a bout of nausea such as she had never experienced before.

Obviously we had more work to do, but I was pleased that Lori was feeling her feelings more. This at least meant that she was in her body, fully participating in the events of her life. Maybe some of it was unpleasant, but she was there.

This time we decided to do a process dealing with her parental influences (I call this a Mother/Father Rollover). It was clear from our first session that Lori had inherited a fear of sex from her mother—it couldn't hurt to explore this further. Both Lori's parents were dead, but this would not affect our work. Like it or not, our parents are with us always as we go through life—not just as memories but as full-blown parts of us with their own beliefs, history and will to survive. In a Mother/Father process I address these parts directly, working to uncover and change their beliefs. The result can be powerful since parent parts tend to be all-pervasive, having a subtle influence on all our parts. When they become more supportive the whole psyche is affected.

Lori's father part presented few difficulties—his love and affection for Lori brought tears of joy to her eyes. It seemed to me that she had idealized him somewhat since his death, but it was through him that she had grown to be warm and caring in spite of the influence of her mother, who was hostile and intractable in the extreme. Her mother part, she said, lived behind a glass wall.

"No one can touch her or get close to her."

"What is the advantage to her of staying behind the glass wall?"

"That's how she cuts herself off from people—and how she inflicts pain on her family."

"What does she accomplish by inflicting pain on her family?"

"It's her way of getting back at her parents. And it gives her a feeling of power."

"Ah. What does power mean to her?"

"Power is in lieu of love. It fills up the void."

"Are there any drawbacks to living behind the glass?"

"She admits that she's lonely—but says it's worth it."

Mother part recalled the humiliation she had felt as an adolescent when her father and brothers began to make sexual advances, as if her developing body made her fair game. All that she believed about sex she had passed on to Lori: *Women are objects … Arousal is bad … Sex is dirty … When they do it to you make sure you feel nothing.*

"Did your mother actually say these things to you?"

"No. My mother never talked about sex."

I understood from this that these beliefs had been transmitted to Lori at a pre-conscious level. And Lori, it seemed, had taken her mother's rules a step further, simply shutting out sex altogether.

Beneath her spiteful exterior, Lori's mother part was riddled with anxiety. She told us that she never left the house and was afraid of being alone at night. She didn't trust people. She felt disliked and ostracized. Fearful, insecure and stuck behind her glass wall, she bore a striking resemblance to the white form that had hidden in the white room. Together, these two parts had made up a big chunk of Lori's psyche—a chunk that was cut off from life and love in the most extreme way.

Lori's mother part was wounded and disillusioned, a classic victim. Seeing herself as helpless and a target she clung to what perverse forms of power she could. For her, the concept of love was linked to being controlled and sexually violated. She was thus unwilling to open herself to either love or sex. Nor was she about to condone her daughter's enjoyment of sex.

Realizing that tact and patience were my only allies, I spent an hour or more dancing around Mother's glass wall, trying to find ways to put her at ease. At one point I asked Lori how she felt about her mother.

"I wanted to love her. I wanted her to love me." Her eyes pooled with tears.

Ask your mother part: "How does she feel about that?"

"She's interested. She's come right up to the glass and is peering through."

"Can she see that you are talking about a different kind of love? Not the kind that controls and violates?"

"Yes—I think she can see that." She covered her face with her hands and began to sob. After a few moments she wiped away her tears and said, "She can see that this love is more powerful."

"Why not teach her the words: My love is powerful."

Lori closed her eyes. "She has a question. What can love-power do for a person?"

"Should I give her an answer?" I asked.

"Yes."

"Well, tell her that strength, creativity and freedom all grow through love. There is a kind of power that comes from resistance but it's very painful and short-lived. The power of love always wins."

This was a turning point for Lori's mother part. Although her resistance did not entirely melt away, she was able to clear out many layers of influence from her own family of origin. In the end, she adopted as her guiding principle: "My power comes from love."

All was well with Mother, but Lori now complained of a "blocked feeling" in her lower abdomen.

"I see something dark, right here between the two chakras." She pointed to a spot on her belly, midway between her base and her navel.

We decided to take a look.

"Ask inside if the part that is creating the darkness will talk to you."

She concentrated for a moment, and then said, "There seems to be more than one part."

In fact, she identified three parts. They had a message for her.

"They say that I'm misusing sexual energy."

"Misusing it how?" I asked.

She squeezed her eyes shut as if trying to focus on an obscure mental image. "I don't know," she whispered. "By harming people or making them feel bad."

"Consciously, do you think you would do that?"

"I don't know. I don't think so."

"Well ask these parts: How do they explain the fact that you don't know what they're talking about?"

Her brow creased. "They say there's a part of me that does misuse sexual energy."

"Can they direct you to the part that is doing that?"

She gave me a haunted look. "Yes, I get a sense of that part."

"Okay. Let's ask that part if it would be willing to communicate."

She paused; then nodded.

"Ask it: How old was I when you were first created?"

"It was with me when I was born."

"And ask it: How, specifically, did I misuse sexual energy?"

"It says by playing on people's emotions." She shuddered and seemed to withdraw into herself. Her expression was dark and furtive, revealing both fear and guilt.

"Do you think you can handle knowing about this?" I asked gently.

"There's something there. It's imageless and dark." She blew out her breath and shook herself but said that she didn't want to walk away from it now and have to dig it up again later. I admired her pluck. And I felt that with her mother part now supporting her she would be strong enough to deal with whatever came up.

"Ask the part what it can show you," I suggested.

"I'm getting some pictures." Her voice was taut and distant. Her eyes roamed beneath flickering lids. "It looks like a dungeon, very damp and cold. There's mold growing on the walls."

"Who's there?" I asked.

"It's me but it's not me. A man."

"Ask the part: What were we doing there?"

"He says: I control this place."

"Interesting. Ask him: How does he feel about this place that he controls?"

"He doesn't like it. It's very cold." She paused. "But he has to do it to survive."

"So he did it for a living?"

She nodded. "He seems to work for long periods of time, and then there's a break. He goes outside and up the stairs into the sunlight."

"How does he feel in the sunlight?"

"It's much better than the cold." In spite of her shallow breathing and ghostly pallor I thought she was calm enough to continue.

"Ask him: How did he get into this job?"

"He was taught very young by someone who did things similar to him."

"And what is it that he does?"

"He says he hurts people." She gave me a despairing look, and then suddenly her hands flew up to cover her eyes.

"What do you see?" I asked.

"It's a dungeon. I saw blood on the walls, but it was just a brief flash."

I encouraged her to stay with it. She let out a long, shaky breath and said, "I smell everything! I see everything! It's not acceptable!"

I decided not to press her for details but asked simply if the dungeon keeper enjoyed hurting people.

"No, he doesn't enjoy it but he has to do his job."

"Does he know what year it is?"

"Fifteen something."

"Is he in the dungeon now or is he in the street?"

"He's in the dungeon but he wants to go home."

"Why not follow him home and see what his home is like."

Lori raked her hands through her hair. "It's awful. He sleeps on straw. It's very dirty. He has a place where he can cook, but it's just a black pit in the ground."

"What else can he tell us about his life?"

She looked at me sorrowfully. "Because of what he does nobody will have anything to do with him. He's ostracized by his community. And he hates himself. He believes he's condemned."

"For how long does he believe he will be condemned?"

"Maybe forever," she said. "He doesn't know how to stop punishing himself."

"Ask this part: What are his religious beliefs?"

After a silence she said, "I'm getting two things. While he's alive he doesn't even think of anything bigger than himself — he has no conscience, no guilt. But after he's passed on he feels terrible remorse for what he's done."

I was intrigued that Lori was seeing the dungeon keeper both during and after his life. I sometimes lead people towards this meta-perspective but had never before seen anyone find it spontaneously.

"Does he know who's talking to him?" I asked.

"He says my voice sounds familiar."

"I'd like you to tell him you're from the new world. That since his time the earth has been found to be a sphere and that you're on a continent called North America."

She shook her head. "He doesn't know how I exist."

"Why not show him? Show him pictures of Arizona, the red sandstone, the cactus, the arroyos — and the cities with their legislative buildings. Tell him that the government here doesn't use torture. That you have the freedom to disagree."

I felt the update to be especially important for this part since his world view was so archaic. He was amazed, even relieved, by all that Lori showed him, and yet he still felt imprisoned in his torture-or-be-tortured reality.

"Ask him what decision he made when he passed on."

"That he would never harm anyone again."

"Can he see that his decision has been carried forth — in that you have not harmed anyone since then?"

Lori looked at me darkly. "But I have harmed since then," she said.

Knowing what a kind and caring person Lori was, this took me by surprise. But it soon became clear that she was referring to yet another previous life. This time she saw herself as a plains native during the European settlement of North America.

"I'm a man again." She gave me a pained look. "I struck out in anger."

"What were you angry about?"

"They killed my wife and child."

"And what did you do?"

"I took revenge."

"Does this man know what caused the attack on his family?"

"It was unprovoked—almost like a killing spree."

"And what decision did he make?"

"He didn't want to be harmed and he didn't want to harm anyone."

"What happened to him after that?"

She concentrated, and then said, "He was very lonely the rest of his life. But it seemed he was a scout. He always went up ahead to make sure that if somebody was going to be harmed it would be him."

"So by protecting others he made up for his vengeance and for his life as a dungeon keeper."

"Yes. I think the dungeon keeper knows that—or at least the part of him that passed over knows it."

Since the dungeon keeper was in two parts, I asked Lori to introduce the part of him that had passed over to the part that was still feeling condemned and ostracized. "Let him know that he did reach the decision not to harm again. Bring that news right into his mind."

Lori closed her eyes. As I waited I could see the tension draining out of her. "That feels much better," she said.

"Now ask him to go back in his memory. Can he recall a time before he worked in the dungeon?"

"He was a child, loved by his mother. He was very trusting."

"What did he know about harm at that time?"

"It didn't exist."

"Ask him to look forward from then. Can he see when harm first entered his life?"

After a pause she said, "It was when he became an instrument of the king. He was fourteen or fifteen."

"Interesting. And what has he learned about harm? Ask him to think about that—both from the perspective of the trusting child and from the perspective of the part of him that passed over."

"He thought he had to do it to survive—but it was just blind obedience. He didn't listen to his own feelings or think for himself."

"And how does he feel now that he's decided not to harm again? Can he trust himself with that?"

Lori paused to think this over. "He's not sure. Because he did kill again as the plains native."

"He did," I conceded. "Though a crime of passion is not the same as a life given to torture and murder."

"But it did happen," Lori said.

"Yes, but even the plains native who killed in anger felt terrible guilt, and then tried to make up for it by protecting others."

"True. It doesn't feel good to kill."

I asked the dungeon keeper to remain in the feelings of trusting and being loved as a child, and to bring those feelings forward through his whole life, allowing them to dissolve the beliefs that led to him doing what he did—the belief that he had to torture or be tortured, that he was forever condemned and that he had no freedom to choose.

"Have him bring that loving, trusting energy all the way through, right to the time of his passing over."

Lori sat in deep concentration. When she finally looked up her eyes were light and far away. "His life is different," she said. "He moves away when he's fourteen or fifteen—goes to live somewhere else. He's happy."

Lori too felt better and on this note we ended the session. Much darkness had been dispelled, and the painful confinement of both the dungeon and Mother's glass prison had been cleared away. I left Lori with an invitation to call me when she felt ready, and as the weeks passed I thought of her often, hoping that she was doing well. It was two months before she was again sitting before me.

"I have good news and bad news," she said.

She told me the good news first.

A few days after the previous session she had initiated sex with her husband.

"And guess what? It worked. There was no pain—none at all." She laughed gleefully. "I couldn't tell which of us was more surprised."

That first breakthrough was just the beginning—she found herself going back for more at every opportunity and felt that her whole life had turned a corner. After ten years of marital celibacy she was finally experiencing the intimacy she had longed for.

And then the curtain fell. Sometime during the fourth week it all came to an end. Not only did her vagina seize up again—as if some "close sesame" command had caused the vault door to slam shut—but her desire left her as well. She felt turned off, disinterested, even slightly revolted by sex.

As far as her sex life went, she felt she was back at square one. But she had noticed something else—an increase in her sensual pleasure. What she ate, what she looked at, smells, sounds, sensations—everything was more "real."

"It's like the world no longer has a dullness over it."

The changes Lori described made sense. The dark spot that we had worked on was close to her base chakra, which powers not just the sex drive but vitality and appetite in general. As I explained to her, when you open sexuality you open all the appetites.

What Lori wanted to work on now was getting back to the tropics of love she had so briefly visited. She had tasted the fruit and could no longer settle for life without it. I asked her to go back to those days when she was feeling aroused and enjoying sex.

"Remember how it felt—some of the sensations."

Her eyes closed and a smile played across her face.

"Now go forward in time to the point when it started to shift, when you began to notice it changing."

"It's like gray clouds. I've already got tears in my eyes."

"Ask inside: Would the part of me that produced those gray clouds communicate with me now?"

"It's really far away."

"Does it want to communicate?"

"I can't! I can't!" Lori whispered, shaking her head.

"Well, tell it thank you for letting us know. And ask it: What's stopping you from communicating?"

"It's afraid of change, of opening up, becoming vulnerable."

"Vulnerable to what?"

"Death." Her voice was barely audible.

"What do you believe death is?"

"Painful."

"What makes death painful?"

"Surprise."

Her expression was so despairing, her eyes showed such alarm, that I paused to ask her what was happening. She said she was picking up an emotion. It was fear. There was sadness there too. Then, in tears, she described the image of a sword going into her body through the vagina. She looked on the verge of being ill.

"Okay, let's break for a minute," I suggested. "Let the part know that it's here with us and quite safe."

I handed her a Kleenex. She wiped away her tears and blew her nose; then told me that the part had been way off in the distance during the period when she was sexually active, but in the end had moved closer in order to protect her.

"How is this part connected to you?" I asked.

"I have the impression of clenching, like when you make a fist."

She held up her hand to demonstrate. "It controls my muscles by making them contract."

As we explored the part's memories and beliefs it mentioned that it had firmed up its control of Lori when she turned sixteen. This was necessary, the part said, because her developing body and sexuality made her vulnerable. Vulnerable to what? To people who might cause her "physical and emotional harm."

"In what way would they do that?" I asked.

Lori seemed confused as she answered.

"It's like being grabbed and dragged off." She paused. "The part sees me being abducted." She put a hand over her eyes and said she felt dizzy.

I assured the part that Lori was in no immediate danger of being abducted. Lori drank some water and after a few minutes said she was feeling better. But when I asked her if she had ever actually been abducted, oddly enough, she seemed uncertain.

"How is your memory of age sixteen and on?" I asked. "Are there any fuzzy areas?"

"Let me think." She pinched the bridge of her nose. "That would be grade ten or eleven. No, I don't remember being abducted. I have a pretty clear memory of that age. Prior to that it's a little fuzzier."

"Prior to that do you think you were abducted?"

She paused to consider. "No, I don't think so. There would have been a big to-do made of it."

"One would think."

"I mean my father would have been very upset if I'd been abducted." She looked thoughtful, uncertain. "I'm trying to think if I really was. Somebody abducted me but I don't know when or where."

She again complained of dizziness; then asked, "Do you think it was in another lifetime?"

"I don't know. Ask the part."

Her brow furrowed, and then cleared. "It says yes."

This at least offered an avenue for exploration — though I was growing wary of her tendency to find understanding through past-life metaphors. I wondered to what degree her parts were simply inventing convenient explanations. I accepted, however, that this was her current way of resolving things.

I asked the part to fill us in on what was happening. Lori described the scene that was in her mind.

"It's night. I'm a woman. I have a white apron on. Two men are holding me — one on either side. They're dragging me backwards."

At this point the part became reticent, saying that it would not continue because it didn't want Lori to relive the pain of that experience. Its job after all was to protect her from it. I agreed with the part and suggested that it simply stop the action. We needed to clarify who Lori was and which life she was living. Accordingly, I asked Lori to make a good clear picture of herself, put today's date on it, and show it to the part.

After a moment she said, "The part can see a beam of light coming out from my heart. It's joining me to the woman who's being dragged."

"So the part can see that you and she are two different people. Make sure it knows that in this lifetime you are not in any danger."

She nodded.

"Can the part see that it might not be appropriate to be controlling and protecting you, even though you may have needed it in another life?"

Her face clouded. "The part is confused," she said.

"Well it would be confused because it's crossing lives. Ask it to think about that." I gave it a moment before continuing. "Now if it can cross lives we can cross lives as well. How would this part feel about us helping the woman in the other life who's being abducted?"

"It's still not sure about showing me that memory. It doesn't want to hurt me in this life."

"Well, tell the part that it is hurting you in this life. Shutting you down and making you incapable of living life fully is a form of hurting."

"I think it's beginning to understand."

The part agreed to let us do what we could to help. But helping was not as easy as I anticipated.

I first asked Lori to send her love along the beam of light that joined her to the captive woman. "And through this beam also send her the strength to break away from her abductors."

Lori gave this her best effort, sending out wave after wave of warmth and energy — but didn't see it making a difference.

"I guess you'll have to go to the scene in person," I concluded. "See if you can project your image to that time and place. I'd like you to just stand there beside her."

"She thinks she's seeing a ghost," Lori laughed. "But she's not frightened. It's almost as if she were expecting me."

"Ask her what is holding her there. What is keeping her from breaking away?"

"She knows that her life is going to be short."

"How does she know that?"

"She planned it."

"Interesting. How old was she when she planned it?"

"It was before she was born."

"And was her life short?"

"Yes. She was killed by these men."

Ask her: "What did she plan to learn from this experience?"

"She wanted to learn compassion — to love others in spite of what they might do to her."

"Did she learn that?"

"Yes. She has no malice. But she has fear."

"So in learning compassion she also learned fear. And that is being transmitted to herself in lives to come."

"She didn't know that."

"Ask her: What, specifically, did she learn to fear?"

"Surprises. Not knowing what's going to happen. She feared the unknown."

"Was she surprised at how she died in that life?"

"Yes. In the end she wasn't ready for it."

I thought we might make better progress if this part was not so frightened and suggested that Lori take her back to a time before the abduction took place. She went back several hours—it was earlier that same day. Now Lori could see her more clearly.

"Her name is Nan. She lives on a farm. She looks an awful lot like me but she wears a long dress and a white apron."

As the eldest girl in a large family, Nan's job was to take care of the other children.

"She works hard but enjoys her life," said Lori. "Her parents are very kind. There's lots of warmth in the house."

"Does she feel safe?"

"She feels safe as long as she's on the farm."

"I'd like her to stay in that feeling of warmth and safety. And from there, to look forward at the events leading up to her abduction."

Lori nodded, though her face was pale.

"Be there with her in the warmth and safety. Hold her hand. And ask her to take a look at the men who are about to abduct her. Can she tell what they were feeling?"

"Anger at the world."

"Can she feel their anger?"

"Yes." Lori was crying now.

"Can she sense what's driving their anger?"

"They have so much fear and pain inside them that they feel compelled to commit terrible acts of violence."

"How does she feel about that?"

"Strange—she felt bad for them. She knew that she would die and she just felt bad for them."

"And how does she feel about the fact that she herself in another body is visiting her right now, coming back to help?"

"She says she wishes she hadn't chosen this kind of an end."

"This is a very difficult way to learn compassion. Would she like to re-choose her end?"

"Can she?"

"Yes. Explain to her that Lori is choosing a different course for herself in this life too."

"She would like to have a different end."

"Well, to do this," I pointed out, "we need to change the core beliefs that precipitated this event. Ask Nan: What does she believe about the world beyond the farm?"

"It's dangerous."

"Where was she when she was abducted?"

"She was out at night alone, walking home from somewhere. I can't tell where."

"So she had fifteen good years, and then she brought that dangerous world to her," I said. "Because according to her beliefs it was inevitably going to happen."

"What do you mean?" Lori asked.

"She believed the world was a dangerous place and she believed that she would have to die violently in order to learn compassion. I would say that anytime she ventured beyond the farm she was at risk of activating those beliefs."

Lori's eyes widened as she took this in. "She really did believe those things."

"And yet, as she said earlier, she was surprised by the turn of events," I commented.

"I guess it wasn't really surprising," Lori said.

"Not really," I agreed. "But I wonder where she learned that the world could be a dangerous place."

"Not from her parents." Lori shook her head thoughtfully. "I don't know. Right up to the time of the abduction her life was happy."

I asked Nan to follow her fear of danger back through time to see if she could locate its origin. It was no surprise when she landed in yet another lifetime.

"I see lots of shiny metal. There's—what do you call that—armor. It looks like a jousting match."

"Armor and a jousting match," I said. "Interesting."

"She's on a horse. She's wearing metal. She can feel the cold of it next to her body. She's male."

"Ask her how it feels to be male."

"She feels afraid but she can't show her feelings."

"So the fear is there but it's hidden. Ask her what choices this man made that brought him to this point in his life."

"He felt that to conquer his fear he had to be the very best at what he did."

"And was he?"

"He was very good."

"Did he harm others?"

"Yes, he killed people. But he was still afraid. Each time he rode into combat he feared it would be his last—that he would die a horrible death."

"Are there other people around?" I asked.

"He's in the middle of a match, riding up and down and holding this long—you know those things. Everything is metal, even his hands are covered in metal. His horse has metal across its face, on its legs. Terribly hard to move like that."

I asked the jouster to look forward through his life and tell us how he met his death. If we were going to help him—and through him, Nan—it was important to consider his life as a whole. He told us that he did not die in combat. His fear drove him to keep his jousting skills and his killing instinct tuned to a lethal pitch.

Not only did he survive, he became renowned for his skill.

"Yet through it all he never lost his fear," said Lori.

I asked him to remember back to his early years in that life, all the way back to when he first learned about jousting. "What beliefs did he hold that made his life what it was?"

"That you have to kill or be killed. That the way you conquer fear is by being stronger than everybody else."

"And what did he decide as a result of how he lived."

"He didn't like killing people. When he struck them he could see the pain in their eyes."

Eventually, said Lori, the jouster went into retirement.

"He felt great remorse for all the killing he'd done and spent his later years punishing himself."

Knowing that in its day jousting was an entirely respectable profession, I was puzzled by his remorse. But I simply asked, "How did he punish himself?"

"He gave up everything he had won and became what looks to me like a bag person. He has no friends and just wanders from place to place, getting food where he can and sleeping outside."

"What an interesting life," I remarked.

Since starting out with Lori's gray clouds we had followed a breathless course, moving through the terror of Nan, who had been run through by a sword, and landing in the life of the jouster, who also feared just such a death. I thought there was a perverse but clear logic in the way these lives had unfolded. The jouster, full of remorse, had gone on to an existence as a farm girl, bringing with him his knowledge of a vicious world where murder was commonplace. And there, his deepest fear was realized when, in the body of Nan, he died by the sword.

I found myself marveling—not for the first time—at the dramas that Lori's parts presented. It was fascinating to find such fear and violence in a person so gentle, and yet it made sense in a way, given the fierce tenacity of her vaginismus.

My immediate plan was to present the jouster with some alternate choices. I asked Lori to project herself into his time and place so that, as he wandered alone through the countryside, she appeared before him as a kind of spirit guide. He wasn't too surprised to see her, she remarked, as he had become "a little fey" by then.

"How do you feel towards him?" I asked.

"I like him. He's a good person."

"Make sure he knows that."

"He wants to be forgiven." She paused. "It's easy to forgive him."

"Ask him to remember back to before he learned about jousting, before he bought the belief that you conquer fear by being the strongest."

Lori brightened as she said, "He's sitting in his mother's lap. She's got her arms around him and she's rocking him."

"How does he feel?"

"Warm, happy—he knows he's loved."

"How does being loved make him feel?"

"Strong."

"Ask him: Can that strength conquer fear?"

"Yes. It's like he knew that—but forgot it."

"Teach him the words, my strength comes from love."

"He likes that." She smiled.

I smiled too. This was similar to the belief that Lori's mother part had adopted in an earlier session: My power comes from love. I'd noticed that many of Lori's parts were involved in power struggles arising from a victim mentality. That we were touching on this theme across a broad base indicated to me that Lori was making a solid shift on a life-script level.

"Now ask him to imagine how his life would have been if he had held onto that understanding."

"That gives him hope," she said.

"Would he like to change the shape of his life?"

"Yes."

"Ask him to bring the knowledge that his strength comes from love all the way through his life, from the beginning to the end. And to use that knowledge to transform the old rules: *you have to kill or be killed … you have to fight to conquer your fear.*"

Through this meditation the jouster's life was transformed. Lori saw him now as a teacher, surrounded by young people asking his advice. I asked her to introduce this wise teacher to Nan.

"Does he have any advice for this young woman who believed she would have a short life that ended in violence?"

Lori said that because the jouster's life had changed, there was no longer any reason for Nan to be killed. She felt safe now, and because she had no fear she could live her life differently.

"How does it turn out?"

"There are no abductors. She marries a young man from a neighboring farm. I see them having a family and growing old together."

"What is she learning from this alternative future?"

"She says that love is stronger than fear."

"Can she trust that?"

"It's given her a better life."

"Amazing how practical love can be," I remarked.

We both laughed.

"Now that Nan is a contented old woman," I continued, "ask her to send her trust in love both to you and to the part that wanted to protect you. Have her bring it through to all levels within you—the physical, emotional, mental and spiritual, dissolving the fear and the belief in fear. Also have her dissolve the rigidity, the clenching and the need to control."

The control part, which had opened the doorway to these dramatic scenarios, was now happy to join with the physical body in

Lori's present life. As the end note of the session, the part proclaimed its new belief that loving Lori (rather than controlling her) would keep her strong and alive.

This, our third session, took place in late November. I thought about Lori through the holidays and wondered how she was doing. By now I had realized that my work with her was not going to be as straightforward as I'd initially thought—but I did feel that we were working our way through significant layers of belief. Little did I realize what major changes were brewing in her life.

She appeared for another session in the first week of January. As she took off her coat she barely looked at me and seemed ready to explode. The moment we were behind closed doors she came out with her story.

After our previous session she had felt a renewal of sexual interest and once again she and Hugh had fallen into a period of blissful lovemaking. Then, one afternoon, Lori got news that blew her world apart. A woman friend, someone Lori liked and trusted, called to say that she had been having an affair with Hugh for some ten years—almost the entire duration of Lori's and Hugh's marriage.

"That bastard lied to me for ten years," Lori raged. "Our entire relationship has been a sham."

"It does make sense that it would come out now," I commented.

"Yes—she was jealous because I was having sex with her boyfriend," Lori replied sardonically.

We spent the session working through her anger and feelings of betrayal and looking at her choices for the future. She believed that the rift between her and Hugh was beyond repair.

"How could I ever trust him again?"

Over the following months Lori got busy making a new life for herself. We talked on the phone occasionally, and I provided what support and encouragement I could as she went through her separation and divorce. Because she had a good job and was not dependent on Hugh for money, the transition was at least not painful on a material level. Before long she was established in her own apartment—and soon after that she had a new beau.

By the time she returned for another session it was again winter. She looked healthy and full of life—it seemed that the changes in her life had done her good. But as she spoke about her new boyfriend she grew anxious. She and André had formed a close bond but she had been unable to consummate the relationship. Each time she tried, the old pain came back. Those brief periods of opening up that she had enjoyed with Hugh now seemed distant and irretrievable. This was all the more upsetting because she loved André and wanted a serious commitment.

Understandably, she felt frustrated—it seemed to her that her body was acting independently of her wishes, making a normal life impossible. She had first come to see me a year and a half earlier, determined to resolve her problem. Now we were embarking on our fifth session and, while many areas of her life had opened up, the progress in her sex life had been sporadic.

I decided this time to call on the part that caused her vaginal contractions, and soon found myself conversing with the vagina itself.

"If I enjoy sex too much Lori might die," said the vagina.

Puzzled, I asked it how the enjoyment of sex would cause death.

"The life force would leak out of the body."

"Leak out how?"

Lori closed her eyes. "I see a flood flowing out of a woman's body through the vagina."

This part, the vagina, had learned from experience that sex and death are linked. "There have been many lives of sudden violent death," it told us.

As always, I focused less on the experiences themselves and more on the decisions the part had made as a result of them. The session went quickly, as did most of my work with Lori. She processed her thoughts and feelings easily and at the same time her insights and resolutions were genuinely profound. Yet it was troubling that she was still consigning all traumatic experience to other times, places and personages. At our next session, therefore, I was pleasantly surprised when her parts remained in her present life.

She still complained of tightness and pain and was still unable to have sex. In short, there had been no improvement after our previous session. But as we chatted, she happened to mention a rather significant detail of her condition that had not come up before. There was something like scar tissue in her vagina, she said—"a hump, very red" that had been noted by doctors and by André as well.

"We have inserted André. He's gotten inside up to where the hump is, and then with no conscious intention on my part, my muscles have pushed him out."

The pain always focused at this one point, and yet she had no memory of being injured in that area. Her doctor thought it possible that the vaginismus itself might have created the scar tissue through repeated contractions of the vaginal wall. But to her this seemed unlikely since she had not provoked those contractions often—very seldom in fact.

She spoke of other troubling symptoms. She'd recently had dreams of being poked on the abdomen and in the vagina with a hard object.

"Just like the dreams I used to have when I was a kid," she said casually—as if this was something she had mentioned before.

When we asked the hump if it would talk to us it readily agreed.

"There's a lot of pain attached to this part," said Lori.

"What pain is attached to it?"

"Physical pain and shock, unexpectedness, having penetration forced on it. It feels so vulnerable." Her eyes filled with tears.

The hump told us that it was first created when Lori was two years old, and that its job, its reason for being, was to "control the feeling of vulnerability."

"How does it do that?"

"By tightening the vaginal muscles. This is the part that does that." Lori seemed surprised. "It's so adamant," she said. "There cannot be an opening up."

"What would happen if there was an opening up?"

"Lori would be hurt—physically and emotionally."

Since the part had been created at age two, I asked it what it knew at that time about hurt and vulnerability. The answer was several minutes coming.

"I just got a brief flash, an image of myself as an infant lying on a table." She paused, barely breathing. "I get a sense of a finger being inserted into my vagina. I can feel my whole body seizing up."

True to her words, she doubled over in her chair. I asked her to take some deep breaths, and then helped her up and walked her around the room for a while before continuing.

"Ask the part if this really happened. Or was it something it thought might happen?"

"Yes, this happened to the baby."

The hump maintained that Lori had been invaded over and over again, always without warning. The shock and physical pain had filled the part with dread. Its defence had been to seize up at any approach to Lori's genital area. Now, decades later, it was still faithfully doing this job.

We explained to the hump that Lori was an adult now and wanted to make her own choices about sex. The part thought about this, and then answered that Lori was sure to be duped because she wasn't good at reading people. It didn't care at all about her desire for intimacy.

"The part thinks it would be safer for me to be alone for the rest of my life," Lori said. "I think that's a crummy idea."

"Let the part know that you did survive and that you're old enough now to speak up for yourself. Ask it to think about that. As an adult you're not nearly so vulnerable physically and you now have the ability to say what you want and what you don't want."

"The part doesn't trust me to speak my mind."

"Why not begin by speaking your mind to the part. Let it know that physical intimacy is something you desire—that you no longer want it shutting down the possibility of penetration."

Lori closed her eyes to give this message to her part. When she again looked up, she told me with a bright look that the part had backed down. "It respects me for telling it what I want," she said.

The problem I was left with was helping the part find a way to relax. Of course it had no inkling how to do this. Its idea of relaxing was to merely ease up on the constriction—to constrict a little less. I thought it might help if the part had some reference point for relaxation, and cast around in my mind for an idea.

"It uses up a lot of energy making tightness. Where does that energy come from, do you think?"

Lori didn't know.

"Ask the part to look back through its history and through all the lives that have added to this constriction. Can it find the source that has sustained it and nourished it through all it has experienced?"

I waited pensively, wondering if this hump, which had been so rigid for so long, would be able to find the open font of energy at its base. Lori took a long time answering. When she finally raised her head she had a dreamy look in her eyes.

"It's just like an opening up," she whispered.

"Follow the feeling of opening up. Where does it lead you?"

"I see a vast lake and a clear, open vista. The earth feels warm and welcoming."

"Try putting your feet in the water."

"The water cares. It's very warm. Anything is possible here."

"Is violation possible?"

She hesitated, and then gave a measured answer. "The harmonious memories are greater than the violations, and the harmonious sensations are stronger."

"Did unexpected things happen?"

"A storm—but you'd always get a sense of it ahead of time. There was a knowledge that nothing is ever an accident—that I'm a part of it too."

"If that knowledge were there all the time, would it be necessary for the part to constrict?"

"Not if I avoided situations where something bad might happen." Lori hesitated. "But I don't think I trust myself enough to do that."

She felt that hers was a pattern developed over many lifetimes, an enduring expectation that she would be violated. She could not trust herself to discern who would harm her and who would not, and so had come to distrust all men. The vaginismus was a manifestation of this—but the central issue, as Lori herself had seen, was mistrust of self. I asked her to think about this.

"Trust of self is the basis of all trust," I said. "I certainly don't advocate blind, unquestioning faith in every person you meet, but rather a trust in your own discernment and your ability to rise to new occasions. Along with this goes an understanding that you can make mistakes—but that you can recover and learn from them."

I pointed out that it was she who must decide there would be greater benefit in trusting than not trusting. "When you trust you may be disappointed—or even betrayed at times. But by trusting you will gain experience—and that will build resilience. With increased trust, not only will your natural timing improve, you will find, oddly enough, that synchronicity and fortunate coincidence become more commonplace."

"I understand," she said. "But I don't know how to trust myself."

"How can you possibly trust yourself until you decide: I will now trust myself—and see what comes of it?"

She thought about it. "Oddly, that makes sense."

"Let's check back with the hump. Does it feel that Lori can be trusted to be a good guide for this organism?"

"Yes."

"In those times when there were no accidents, how did the part handle lovemaking?"

"By just allowing it to happen. It assumed things would go right and they did."

"What do you think would be the consequence if you allowed this degree of trust in your life now?" I asked.

To her credit she could think only of benefits: Her sex life would improve, her relationship with André could proceed and she would be able to enjoy the intimacy of a close sexual bond.

"Back then, the part trusted its ability to sense when something was about to happen. Ask the part if it could bring that trust and ability to the forefront of Lori's life."

She nodded, closing her eyes.

"And as the part comes through time," I continued, "let it use its open, trusting energy to dissolve all the old doubts and fears, the expectations of violation, the decision to protect myself, not to trust myself, images of rape—through all the lives and in all the parts of the body."

The room was so silent that I could hear both of us breathing. When Lori at last looked up, her eyes were clear and bright.

"How does the part feel now?"

"Wonderful."

"Is it willing to trust Lori and support her choices about sex?"

"Yes."

I asked her to visualize her vagina and tell me what it looked like in her mind's eye. It seemed wider and softer than before, she said. Not rubbery as she used to imagine it. The hump was different too—it had lost its dark reddish tint and was now pink like the tissue around it.

"There's a softness there that I've never felt before. A receptive feeling. It's kind of strange and new."

"Does the vagina recognize that this is its natural state?"

"Yes."

"Does it feel respected?"

"Yes. It feels that it's been given something it should have had all along."

As this, our sixth session, came to a close, I felt that we had made real progress. I kept my fingers crossed, and a few days later Lori called to say that she and André had at last consummated their relationship. She kept in touch over the following months to let me know that she was enjoying a spring and summer of full-blown lust. As she herself put it: "I'm truly horny for the first time in my life. I have opened up totally."

In late July Lori and André were married, and soon afterwards Lori discovered that she was pregnant. They deliberated about whether to keep the child and in the end decided that they weren't ready to take on this important responsibility. An abortion followed, and after that Lori began to have some recurrence of vaginal pain during intercourse. This happened only intermittently—mainly at times when her marriage was not going smoothly—in other words, when she felt tense and uncommunicative. And the pain was slight compared to its former intensity.

I had known Lori for four years, and altogether we had undertaken six sessions. On the whole, she was so much better (not only had her sex life improved, she was also doing well in her career) that we might have considered our work done and the story ended. In fact, for two years after that sixth session I didn't hear from her at all. Then, on a summer day, she called out of the blue saying she was ready for some followup work. As a result of our session with the hump she had started to wonder about her childhood. Hazy memories were haunting her—thoughts, images and dreams that seemed to spring from a long-forgotten past.

We undertook three sessions in a six-month period, each time working with parts that constricted. Lori was now firmly rooted in her present life—not quite believing what her parts were telling her, yet willing to face the possibility that it could be true. All her memories of violation dated to infancy. The parts that remembered these incidents pointed the finger at an uncle who had been in the family circle till Lori was five. Her fear and pain, her vulnerability, her anger and frustration at being helpless to stop what was happening to her—all these feelings were lodged in the vagina itself and in related parts that were still trying to prevent penetration, still convinced that sex was the worst thing that could happen to her. According to the parts, their job was to "never forget so it will never happen again."

Many of the images that arose in these sessions were hard for Lori to handle.

"The part remembers somebody pulling on my bedclothes, rolling me over on my back. I'm struggling to get away but I'm pinned."

The same part described a feeling of being poked in the vagina with a metal object. This particular memory came up again and again, with more details gradually filling in. The culprit was finally identified as Lori's older sister. The metal object was a spoon.

"It's a mindless, insensitive curiosity. It's not malicious, but it's like I'm not even human."

Lori felt that the uncle had put the sister up to it, though most of her memories implicated the uncle alone. She saw herself lying on her back getting her diaper changed, the uncle pawing at her genitals and inserting a finger into her vagina.

"I feel my whole body seizing up. I never knew when it was going to happen. I want to get off the table but I can't move."

On another occasion, she said: "I'm naked on the table. He's drunk. I'm being touched all over my body, held down on my chest and stomach. It happened many times."

"How many times did it happen?"

"Maybe twenty or thirty times."

When I asked her what decision these events had led her to make, she said, "This will never happen to me again." Or alternatively, "There's no enjoyment in being female."

Both Lori and her parts believed that the uncle was capable of killing her in one of his drunken rages, which he was well known for. This at least offered a present-life rationale for her persistent association between sex and death.

We did specific healing on the abuse memories. In each case I asked Lori to put herself in the memory and stop what was happening. On one occasion she spontaneously whacked her uncle over the head with a baseball bat. Shocked and incredulous, he staggered backwards out of the room.

"He won't show his face around here again," she said with satisfaction.

In spite of all this, Lori did not consciously believe that she had been sexually abused as a child.

"How can it be true?" she protested many times. "This couldn't have happened to me. How could I possibly remember it? — I was too young."

I was glad that she had the sense to question her parts' reports, but reminded her that she had not questioned her past-life memories.

"My skepticism seems to be selective," she said with a smile.

"True. And you may never know the actual facts," I told her. "But this is not about confronting family members. Our goal here is to find and change beliefs — and your subconscious imagery is helping us to do that."

Lori underwent dramatic changes after these final sessions. She found herself wanting sex more and enjoying it without reservation. Only when she had sex just to please her husband was there any constriction. Unlike most women, Lori did not have the option of faking sexual pleasure.

Two years after our final session Lori's marriage with André broke up, though not due to sexual problems. After that, she and I exchanged occasional e-mails, with her reporting that she was happy and involved in her work. When I inquired about her sex life, she answered, "I really don't know the status of the vaginismus because I haven't been in a sexual relationship since André and I separated." But she went on to say, "I do know that vaginismus will never be a barrier again—it's just a question of feeling connected and safe with the person I'm with."

Not as definitive as I would have liked—but fair enough. Then, several months later, I received another message from Lori, filled with news about a promotion at work. And in a discreet postscript, she added, "By the way, I have enjoyed some wonderful amorous sessions with a man I met at a conference—with no hint of pain."

———————

Working with Lori was never dull. Her processing was fast-paced and dramatic—all the more so because she slipped so easily into highly emotional "past-life" dramas. While these were engaging, I knew they might well be symbolic. I am quite willing to believe that we do reincarnate and that we have the ability to look into our other existences, but I do not assume that every image of a distant time and place arises from another life. And whether such imagery is historically accurate or merely metaphorical has not proved relevant to getting results in my work. The same holds true for abuse memories. Most significant from my perspective are the beliefs that are actively affecting someone's life.

Oddly enough, I've found that chronic pain and mysterious physical symptoms (such as Lori's) often do evoke bizarre images and metaphors. Most physical symptoms develop outside the conscious realm, where the processes that create them are separate from our everyday perception. For this reason the parts associated with these physical symptoms may not know the answers. Caught in the complexities of a disease process, they will grasp at whatever explanations they can, producing images that reflect the feelings and beliefs they are contending with. Oftentimes these images may seem to come from past lives or childhood abuse. True or not, they reflect actual feelings and beliefs. Thus, it is my policy to work with them as given at a psychological level. (I consistently discourage clients from confronting family members or taking legal action based on this kind of unsubstantiated information.)

There is also the possibility that what Lori's parts showed her was true. Let's say that she actually did have a series of lives in which she decided and re-decided that she did not want to torture or kill. She comes into her present life with this decision in place — and yet the beliefs that she held as a jouster and dungeon keeper remain unchanged: You have to torture or be tortured, kill or be killed. So she does follow through on her decision not to harm, but the fearful beliefs persist. If all our incarnations are happening simultaneously, as metaphysical philosophers claim, then the shift of a core belief in one life will have a significant effect on other lives in which there are resonating core beliefs. By changing her beliefs Lori was able to resolve her karma concerning harming and being harmed.

As we have seen, Lori herself was skeptical about much of what her parts presented, sometimes protesting that she was just "making up" the answers to my questions. Her doubts may have been well founded, but in my approach to therapy answers must come through the imagination. This is really the only option given that my inquiries are along the lines of: If your illness could speak, what would it say? If your vagina could speak, what would it say? Imagination is a powerful tool and though it may lead us away from fact it can provide rich and viable metaphorical imagery. As Lori's story demonstrates, imagination is sometimes the only means we have of tapping into a deeper understanding of ourselves and the world.

And so, to Lori—one of the many who have asked me, "How do I know I'm not making this up?"—I gave my usual reply:

"You probably are making it up. And that's okay."

Meltdown

It's easy to assume that a person who lies in bed from one month to the next claiming to be too tired to move is imagining or at least exaggerating her symptoms. To the uninformed, myalgic encephalomyelitis (like its cousin, chronic fatigue syndrome) can look a lot like hypochondria. Those who suffer from it experience a bewildering array of symptoms, and yet an uninformed doctor is not likely to find anything seriously wrong.

The mystery around these illnesses persists partly because their medical correlates were not clearly identified until the mid 1980s. They are now believed to be viral-immunological diseases — caused by a virus and associated with a defective immune system. Confusion is also due to there being many such tired diseases (as I refer to them), all closely related. As well as myalgic encephalomyelitis (ME) and chronic fatigue syndrome (CFS), there is chronic fatigue immune dysfunction syndrome (CFIDS) and fibromyalgia, not to mention post-viral, post-toxic, post-immunization and post-traumatic brain syndromes.

When Lydia came down with ME in 1989 there were still very few doctors who knew anything about it, and so, like many others with the disease, she was subjected to a full course of intolerant attitudes and bad advice. When she finally found a doctor who could diagnose her, he told her that she was a textbook case.

Her condition began typically with a flu-like illness. After several days of rest she began to feel better and returned to her job as chief physiotherapist at a large rehabilitation clinic. Within a day or two, however, her symptoms returned full force. She was sent home to bed and there she stayed, falling into a profound depth of illness.

The degree of fatigue experienced by ME sufferers is hard for the ordinary healthy person to grasp. One patient likened it to having a cannonball lodged in the pit of her stomach. During the first year of her illness Lydia could barely summon even the strength to speak.

Because the virus associated with ME affects the brain, it can have repercussions for the entire body and its many interrelated functions, including the motor, sensory and cognitive abilities. Lydia's depth perception was off and she had difficulty coordinating her limbs and keeping her balance. She walked into doors. Getting from her bed to the bathroom required a major effort of focus and persistence.

"I have to look at my feet to know they exist and look at the ground to know it exists. Walking is a process of finding my foot and thinking, lift it up; then figuring out what lift means and actually causing the body to lift the leg; then thinking what forward means and moving it forward; then thinking what down means to get it down; and then making sure that it's actually on the ground and I'm stable."

She experienced impaired memory and concentration as well. Reading was impossible. As she explained it: "There are days when I can't understand what the shapes mean; there are days when I don't know what the words mean." When she tried to speak she often forgot what she wanted to say.

A lot of pain and discomfort also comes with ME. Lydia suffered from sensitivity to noise and light, inflamed muscles and joints, muscle weakness, fluid retention and lymphatic swelling. Her hands were so swollen at times that she couldn't peel an orange. She was always cold and wore long underwear even in summer. Her sleep was fitful. She had allergic reactions to a wide range of foods and household products.

Unfortunately, even after she was correctly diagnosed, her doctor could provide little help. The best he could do was treat individual symptoms with things like anti-inflammatories, pain-killers and sleeping pills. These could ease some of the pain and distress, but there was no treatment for the disease itself.

The good news, she learned, was that ME is not progressive: There would not be irreparable damage and with luck she would improve over time. But how much improvement over how long, no one could say. Few of those stricken ever regain their previous level of health, and some remain bedridden for life.

When Lydia and I met for our first session, she had been ill for six years. During that time some of her functional ability had returned, though this was partly due to experience—she had learned to manage her symptoms and avoid the stress and exertion that could cause relapses. On the whole, however, her prognosis did not look good. As she explained to me: "If the disease holds on for longer than a year or two, then it's going to be with you for life." All the same, she had not given up hope.

"I believe there might be an end to this, given the work we are embarking on."

We began on a Saturday morning in June. To prepare for the anticipated energy drain of our session, Lydia had rested for three days and planned to spend a further three days recovering. Her husband, Alfie, brought her to my door, and I planned to drive her home when we were done.

A middle-aged woman with blue eyes and gray hair, Lydia was small in stature and serious in her manner. She had grown up in a large Catholic family in rural Ontario—her mother British, her father French Canadian. On first impression I found her a little prim, but later realized that the years of illness had taken away her spark and left her with an aura of reserve. To Lydia, this loss of vitality was deeply disturbing.

"I don't have that driving energy to do things when I get up in the morning. I feel I've lost my passion for life."

My opening move was to find out what getting well would mean to her.

"If you could choose to be miraculously healed and suddenly have all your energy back, would you want that?"

She stared at me, and then laughed, admitting it was a dilemma. Of course she was fed up with the illness and would give anything to be rid of it. On the other hand, she deeply feared a return to the grinding routine that had been her life in the years before the illness.

"At the clinic my normal work day was twelve to sixteen hours. Not only was I loaded down with administrative work, I was on several committees and taking night courses as well. On top of that, there were bitter struggles going on between staff and management, and I was usually monkey in the middle."

"Did you give any thought to changing jobs?"

"As I look back, no, that never occurred to me. I never asked myself if it was worth it—not even when I started having stress blackouts."

I could see that, for starters, Lydia needed to build up her trust in herself. She had to believe that, once well, she would be able to create a lifestyle that she could actually inhabit. I had a distinct feeling that, until we could tip that balance, her illness was not going anywhere.

For the moment, I decided, we would take things slow and easy. Rather than immediately calling on a disease part we'd begin with a Mother/Father Rollover—a process that I use to look into parental overlays and heal the ongoing effects of childhood influences. I offered the usual preamble.

"I'm going to ask you some questions and I'd like you to report the first response that comes to mind."

She nodded and waited expectantly, hands folded in her lap,

legs crossed at the ankles.

"Ask inside if the part of you that represents your father's energy will speak with you in consciousness."

She barely hesitated. "Yes."

"How does he represent himself to you?"

"He looks stern. He's just a little guy but he sure makes up for it." Before I could ask another question, she rolled her eyes and said, "He's reminding me that there's a right and a wrong way of doing everything."

"What things?"

"Anything at all. Jogging, cooking, plumping pillows, polishing shoes, small talk, social niceties. I see him strutting around the house inspecting what everyone is doing."

"What does he think of what everyone is doing?"

"Oh, it's invariably wrong. He wants us all to start over again and do it his way—no questions asked. Anyone who questions him gets a backhanded slap across the face." She paused, her color rising. "I was the recipient of Dad's slap often, as were all my brothers and sisters."

"Ask your father part: What does he believe about life?"

"Life should be lived in a disciplined fashion. Everyone must make a contribution."

"What does making a contribution mean to him?"

"Service to family and community. You fill your day with useful activity."

A further cause of friction was Father's old-fashioned morality. Lydia and her sisters were not allowed to look at the daily papers until he had clipped out whatever articles and advertisements he deemed unsuitable for young female eyes.

"As we grew older we became increasingly unwilling to put up with Dad's tyranny. As a result, there was always yelling and arguing in the house."

We next talked to Lydia's mother part and found that she too advocated hard work and self-denial. She said things like, "Every good Christian must practice self-sacrifice" and "You must always put someone else's needs ahead of your own."

I was intrigued when mother part revealed that ME was not Lydia's first experience with long-term illness: As a teenager, she had been bedridden for a year with mononucleosis. Probing a little, I discovered that the illness was preceded by a prolonged battle between Lydia and her mother over the issue of career choice.

"My mother wanted me to go to teachers' college, and I was not about to do that. Two of my older sisters were teachers and I could see that their work never ended. After spending all day at school, their evenings and weekends would be taken up marking papers and preparing lessons."

Lydia's career dream was acting, but she had allowed herself to be talked out of that on the basis that making a living at it would be too difficult.

"If I couldn't act professionally, I was at least going to have some free time to attend workshops and participate in amateur productions."

The argument with her mother went on for months, and only when she came down with mononucleosis was it finally dropped. Now, looking back, Lydia saw that she had made an all-too-expedient escape from teachers' college. She even suggested the possibility that she had created the illness for just that purpose. I was impressed by this insight.

"Ask Mother to look inside Lydia: Is there a part of her that responds with illness when she's not listened to?"

"There's a very small, quiet part that's tired."

It seemed we had awakened this part from a deep sleep—as I asked it questions Lydia rubbed her eyes and yawned. But our attention energized the part and it was soon telling us how it had reveled in the year spent in bed as a teenager.

"The peace and quiet were like heaven."

"How did Mother respond?" I asked Lydia.

"She liked the fact that I was docile for a change. She made it clear that she would do whatever needed to be done. In fact, I had the feeling she was almost encouraging me to stay in bed."

"Ask your mother part if she wanted you to get well."

"She wanted me to have the time to myself that she never had."

I addressed Lydia's mother part directly. "That's interesting — because if Lydia takes this time for herself, doesn't that mean she isn't practicing the self-sacrifice you've tried to teach her?"

"Yes — but Lydia is sick."

"So it's okay to put your own needs first if you are sick?"

"Of course. If you're sick then you have no choice."

This looked to me like a recipe for illness, and I worked with both the tired teenager and the parent parts to show them the consequences in Lydia's later life. As we took the parents to a rollover, their attitudes softened and opened. In the end they agreed to stop dictating to Lydia and to support her in her choices.

I was relieved when Lydia made it through the session without becoming exhausted or losing her concentration. I thought that things had gone well but suspected we had quite a way to go — considering the long duration of Lydia's illness and the sheer number of her symptoms. At least she had gained a good understanding of the agenda she had inherited from her family, and now had parent parts who were supporting rather than undermining her freedom of choice.

Over the next six months we met twice more. We devoted one session to Lydia's insomnia, reasoning that if she slept better she would have more energy. In this session we worked with a part that was intentionally staying awake at night for fear that a sudden health crisis might strike either Lydia or her husband. When we showed this wakeful part how tired Lydia was, it agreed to hand its job over to a watcher, a non-physical part that didn't need to sleep. Knowing the watcher was on duty the wakeful part was at last able to relax. In the end, it agreed to take on the job of creating deep, peaceful sleep—a job it had done for Lydia at an earlier time in her life.

It wasn't until our third session that we finally got around to working with the disease itself.

"Ask inside if the part in charge of the ME would be willing to communicate with you in consciousness."

"Yes. It's a heavy, leaden feeling. There's a lot of resentment attached to it."

"What does the part resent?"

"A lack of time for self. A lack of appreciation for self."

"What did its resentment lead it to do?"

"Shut me down. Cut me off from the world."

The part explained its reasoning: If Lydia was marooned, with no access to the outer world, she would be forced to pay attention to her own needs—"to listen with her inner ear."

"Does the part realize how sick it's made you?"

"No. It has no idea."

"Show it what happened to you six years ago – how you lost all contact, not just with the world but with yourself as well. How you've had less choice than ever before."

"It says that it meant to shut me down somewhat but not completely. It just wanted me to reassess things."

"Is the part aware of the reassessments you've made since you've been sick?"

"No."

"I'm curious. Why would it do this to you, and then not pay attention?"

"Good question."

"What does it have to say about that?"

"It's got its back turned and its arms crossed."

"Ask it what that means."

"It's angry that I let things go as far as they did."

I wanted to find out specifically what the part had shut down, so we asked it for an itemized list. Lydia took a moment to reflect.

"The first thing it shut down was input. By this it means my ability to understand spoken and written language."

"How did it go about doing that?"

The part presented an intriguing visual metaphor. "It would be as if I put my hand between two electrical contacts to disrupt them," Lydia explained. "But the part used tiny sheets of cloth."

She saw these as small squares of red gauze inserted in strategic locations throughout parts of her brain, disrupting the flow of information.

The part had also shut down "processing." It had done this by painting a "green coating" over some of the nerves in her brain and neck. With this coating it had hoped to desensitize Lydia — to create some quiet so that she would be able to think. Ironically, this was what had caused her to lose contact with her inner world.

"It's a botched attempt," Lydia said sternly. "The part doesn't understand the effect of what it's been doing."

Knowing that the part was angry with her, I ventured to ask if its motive had been to punish her.

"No, it only wanted to shake me up and force me to take time for reflection."

"Where did the part learn that making you sick was a good way to do this?"

She stared across the room, her eyes a deep ocean blue. "It was when I was sick with mononucleosis."

"Is this part responsible for the mono?"

"No, but it admits to seeing good things come of it." The good things were peace and quiet, attention from Mother, and time for study and reflection. "I spent a very enjoyable year working my way through the *Encyclopaedia Britannica*."

I informed the part, in case it had not already got the message, that in her present condition Lydia was too sick to do any reading or thinking. To Lydia, I said, "Let the part know that sickness is not acceptable to you as a way to get time or attention."

"It says that it didn't want to cause this."

"Ask it again: What was its intention?"

"It wanted me to honor myself and the richness of myself. To pay attention to the things that are true."

"And yet it would seem that the part has done just the opposite. It cut you off from yourself."

"It's quite unhappy about that. It apologizes."

"Do you accept the apology?"

"Yes."

Getting into the spirit of apology I thought to ask Lydia, "Would you like to apologize to the part for ignoring it for so long?"

She nodded and after a moment said, "I've promised it that I'll never deny it again, no matter what. It wants to repair the damage it's done but it doesn't know if that's even possible."

"Let's find out if it's possible."

I asked the part to turn its attention to the gauze pieces it had placed in Lydia's brain. "What would be the consequence of removing them? Would it be too big a shock? Or would it simply allow things to return to normal?"

The part thought that only good could result and was eager to get started. It thus began the process of going through the brain and pulling out the pieces, one by one. At length, Lydia reported that they were all out and had been stacked in a little cart.

"Let's wheel the cart out through your ear and put it on this table for safekeeping."

The part now eagerly volunteered to dissolve the green coating it had painted over certain nerves. When that was done I asked it to check the connections in the brain to make sure they were all properly re-established. Lydia's closed eyes flickered as this delicate operation proceeded. At last she drew in a deep breath.

"How are you feeling?" I asked.

"Way more centered in myself," she answered, but looked doubtful. When I probed a little, she admitted to feeling nervous.

"It's a nervousness that goes back to other people's expectations. If I get well, then I will again have to do what is expected of me."

But even as she said this she made the classic rude hand gesture.

"Put the finger to that one," I agreed.

We both laughed.

"Yet there is an element in this part of protecting you from other people's expectations," I commented.

Now I returned to the heaviness that Lydia had described on first calling up the disease part. "What are the thoughts or beliefs within that heavy feeling?" I asked.

"It's that same old stuff. Family pressure, Dad's threats — you know." She spoke with weary resignation.

"Ask the part if any of this heavy energy originates with Lydia."

"No."

"Would the part like to be free of it?"

"Yes."

I asked Lydia to project a trash receptacle into the room and to direct her part to lift the heaviness out of itself and place it in the receptacle.

"And along with the heaviness, tell it to put out all the pressure of other people's expectations — and all the resentment attached to that."

Lydia seemed to drift into another dimension. When she finally opened her eyes, they were clear and deep, like still water.

"How is the part feeling?"

"Lighter — and a lot calmer."

"Are those gauze pieces still piled in the little cart?"

"No, they went into the trash as well."

"Should we still call this part a disease part?"

"No."

"What does the part feel is its natural function now that it's lighter and calmer?"

She described the image that came vividly to mind. "I see a small child playing with colored blocks. She's enthralled — not just with the shapes and colors but with her own creative power."

"What is the feeling of that?"

"Pure joy."

"How does pure joy feel?"

"Like growing a thousand arms that are reaching out in all directions."

I couldn't help but notice that Lydia appeared rather stiff and sober as she described the part's radiant energy.

"Are you consciously feeling this joy that the part is feeling?" I asked.

"I feel it here," she said, touching her chest.

"Do you feel it at the same intensity as the part feels it?"

"It's stronger in the part."

I explained that there was little use in the part feeling intense joy unless Lydia could share it. The part had gotten out of touch with her. As a disease part it hadn't realized it was hurting her, and now it needed to remember how to make her feel good.

"Ask the part if it can spread the joy through your body so that you too can feel its full impact."

Within seconds she brightened.

"I'm tingling all over," she said.

I often find that a part's original job is much the opposite of what it's been doing. And so I was pleased, though not surprised, to learn that the disease part had been a joy part in its original state.

Lydia and I kept in touch over the following months and she reported that her health was improving — not just in one area but across the board. She was sleeping better, had more energy and was more focused. Christmas came and went and she chalked up her first winter with no serious setbacks. She was by no means back to normal but she was now able to go out to dinner occasionally and even do a little traveling with her husband. She read an entire novel for the first time since getting sick, and even enrolled in a creative writing course.

Nearly two years passed before I saw her again. I opened the door to her on a bright October morning, noting that she looked remarkably well. I was pleasantly surprised to hear that she had driven herself to the session.

We began with a health review. I wanted to pinpoint exactly how far she had come in her recovery, and how far she still had to go — not an easy task with a disease as insidious as ME. We considered each of her symptoms individually. She thought that most had abated to some degree. When I asked her to rate her overall improvement on a scale of zero to ten, with ten representing perfect health, she gave me the following assessment.

• When the illness first struck eight years before she was at zero.

• Six years later, when we began our work, she was at two.

• Six months after that, following our initial three sessions, she was up to four.

• Since then she had remained stable at four.

Thus, in her own view, she had gained as much during the period of our three initial sessions as she had during the first six years of her illness. And while she was pleased with this progress, I myself experienced a moment of disappointment. I didn't say so but I had hoped for more. It now crossed my mind that even if we could resolve the psychological components of Lydia's disease, she might not rally much at the physical level. Viruses are notoriously tenacious and the virus associated with ME has a reputation for devastating comebacks. I've known people with this disease to regain their health and resume a normal life, only to be laid flat with a relapse. I could only hope that such relapses had less to do with the virus than with psychological saboteurs — parts that are, for whatever reason, invested in the status quo of being weak and sick. These, at least, we could contend with.

When I asked Lydia what had prompted her visit after such a long break, she said, "Frustration with myself for not doing the things that make me feel better."

I asked her to explain.

"I have a game plan," she said. "I've worked hard to look at what food I need and what exercise is best for me. I can walk, I can stretch gently, I can take hot baths, I can eat well — so why am I not doing these things?"

"Well, perhaps some part of you doesn't like your game plan," I suggested. "I'm wondering if your game plan is really taking you into consideration."

The game plan, as it turned out, had no built-in downtime. Even now, emerging from serious illness, she was falling into her old habit of filling every minute of the day with productive activity. I asked her what downtime meant to her.

"Watching TV or putting my feet up and reading. But these are things I have an in-built resistance to. I've been struggling with that for a long time."

"Some people would call that lazy."

"Yes, and it was considered lazy when I was growing up. I was taught that every other person came before myself. The rule was that if you had free time you used it to help someone. Outside of study and school work, even reading was considered a sinful indulgence. To this day, if I'm lying down reading and I hear Alfie coming up the stairs, my first reaction is to jump up and hide the book. I stop myself, of course, but it's that automatic."

"So you don't allow for downtime," I said. "How can you start to allow for downtime, I wonder? Because you're taking it anyway."

"Yes I am. It's so silly."

We used the session to clear out this and other childhood ghosts, allowing her to operate with a more flexible and humane game plan. Then I asked a question I had asked before, but one I considered important.

"If you woke up tomorrow and found yourself completely well, would you be able to live life according to your own choices — without getting caught up in other people's expectations?"

She was now able to answer this question with a tentative yes.

At our next session two weeks later she brought up a surprising new problem.

"I've always had a very bad temper. When it blows I lose it completely — and it's not just a case of throwing things against the wall. I actually become physically dangerous."

I looked appraisingly at the petite figure seated before me.

"Don't doubt it," she said. "I was brought up in self-defense. I studied judo from the time I was six."

She cited several incidents that illustrated her point, beginning with the time a classmate in public school had tangled a sticky lollipop in her hair.

"I grabbed him and gave him a slap. I was totally enraged."

That same rage had reared its head each time her father had given her one of his backhanded slaps, though on those occasions she didn't dare strike back — or at least not until she was older.

"I settled the score with my father when I was fifteen. We were quarreling about something — I can't remember what — and he slapped me a couple of times. I remember Mom saying to him: 'Don't. You've pushed her too far.' I finally took a slug at him and we got into a fist fight. In the end, I flattened him." She paused and added, "It happened in front of the whole family." A glint of pride appeared in her blue eyes.

On another occasion, while she was still at her job, she'd gotten into a scuffle at work.

"A teenage boy, the brother of a patient, brought some snowballs into my office and started pitching them at me. I suppose he was just having fun, but the inside of the snowballs was ice. I kept saying, 'Okay Kevin, that's enough now,' but he wouldn't listen, and finally one of the snowballs ripped the top off a cold sore I had at the time. There was blood gushing from my lip, but even then he didn't stop."

She continued the story with a grim look on her face.

"I'm afraid I lost my temper. I grabbed him by the belt and the scruff of the neck and threw him over my shoulder. I waited till he landed and then left the room to try and cool off. As I was walking down the hall I felt someone touch my shoulder from behind. Assuming that Kevin had come after me I dropped to one knee, reached behind me to grab a belt and an arm, and threw him over my head. But as he went sailing down the hallway I saw that it wasn't Kevin after all but a colleague who was actually a good friend."

As the story thus ended, Lydia and I sat staring at one another wordlessly.

"What worries me," she said finally, "is that I lose control. When I get like that I don't realize what I'm doing."

One of the things that could set her off was noise.

"There's a gang of children who play in the street outside my house. If they get really noisy I actually have to leave the premises and go to the grocery store or the post office to prevent myself from physically attacking them."

She described a movie she had once seen, in which a man had murdered some people for making too much noise. "What frightened me was the depth of empathy I felt for him."

Her rage part, when we called on it, appeared as a strong, quiet woman seated at the head of a conference table.

"She has an imperious air about her, as if she owns the world," said Lydia with disapproval.

The part had a cohort—an older woman who sat to one side nervously chewing a pencil and rustling some papers. When we asked the nervous one what was bothering her, she said that she was upset because Lydia didn't have a job. "Without a job," she declared, "Lydia is worth nothing—to herself or anyone else."

"She's practically shaking with nervous energy," Lydia remarked.

"What is your purpose as a part of Lydia?" I asked the part.

"I'm the organizer. I get things done."

"Are you aware of the changes Lydia has been making in recent years, particularly the increase in her self-respect?"

A little huffy, the part replied, "I've been paying attention. Don't think I'm deficient in my job."

But the organizer didn't think Lydia's inner growth was of much importance. In her opinion, what Lydia really needed was direction—to figure out what she was going to do with her life, and then get on with it.

The rage part, on the other hand, was involved with power.

"Power to do what?" I asked it.

"I'm the man. I get done what I want to get done."

"And what do you want to get done?"

A silence ensued. Finally Lydia said, "She's very still. She seems upset about something."

A memory floated to the surface.

"I see myself as a very small girl, crouched under the stairs. Mom's yelling at me. I'm trying to say my bit but I'm not being heard. She's treating me like an idiot. She thinks I'm too little to understand."

Lydia's features betrayed no emotion but I noticed that she, like her part, had grown still.

"At first I start to cry," she continued. "But then, as Mom walks away, I get very quiet and stubborn."

"What have you decided?"

"That Mom has broken the connection between us."

"What did you decide to do about it?"

"I see myself standing there like an immovable rock."

"What does it mean to be like an immovable rock?"

"It's a narrowing of focus. I'm unmoving and uncaring, so the noise and confusion simply splash up against me. It's a feeling of cutting myself off—from myself and the world."

"This sense of being cut off from yourself and the world is one of the symptoms of your illness," I remarked.

"That's true," she agreed. "Though I haven't been aware of creating that consciously."

I was curious to know what maturity level this rage part had reached. When I asked her how old she felt inside herself, her answer was "ten."

"Has she grown at all since Lydia was ten?"

"I don't think so."

"And yet, she appeared to you as a grown woman at a conference table."

"The woman is the child's projection of what she wants to be when she grows up."

It wasn't a very realistic projection, Lydia added. The part looked a lot like Mortitia from the *Addams Family* TV series: tall and reedy with black hair and long painted fingernails.

"I'd like her to take a look at the real grown-up Lydia, sitting in the chair here. How does that compare with her projection?"

"She's laughing."

"What is she laughing at?"

"Compared to the real thing her projection is ludicrous."

"Interesting. And what does this child of ten look like?" I asked.

"Thin and gangly. She's wearing a plaid dress and there's a ribbon holding her hair in a topknot. She's pouting like a *petit démon*."

I could see that my main task with this part would be to re-establish her link with Mother. This, I thought, would go a long way towards resolving her anger and restoring some inner peace. I asked Lydia to once again take the part back to the time under the stairs when she decided that her connection with Mother was broken.

"I want you to hold her hand while the two of you follow Mom around for a few days. Ask the part to notice what Mom does and how she feels."

Lydia nodded, closing her eyes. "Mom is tired. She's so over-worked."

"Anything else?"

"I can see that she really does care about me. The problem is there's just not enough of her to go around."

"Is there not enough of her or not enough time?"

"What an interesting distinction."

"How does the part feel about that?"

"She's smiling. Shc's remembering the times when Mom paid her some special attention."

"Good for her," I said. "This part has based her life on a broken connection with Mother. And if she realizes just this one thing, that the connection with Mother is not broken, that will be a big change."

"She's only willing to have a connection with Mother through me," said Lydia.

This, to me, was a good sign—it meant that the part gave authority to Lydia rather than Mother, which was as it should be. All that needed to be done was for Lydia to complete the circuit between the little girl and her mother. I opened my mouth to make this suggestion but Lydia was a step ahead of me.

"The three of us are sitting down to tea," she said.

But the tea party was barely underway when Lydia scowled and said, "The little girl has her hands over her ears because there's so much noise. It's all the yelling and arguing between Dad and my older brothers."

"Has this part ever had peace and quiet?"

"Only since I've been sick."

"Interesting. Has she enjoyed that peace and quiet?"

"Yes, damn her! She knows what price I've paid for it and she doesn't care."

I waited as her gaze moved around the room. Finally, she said, "I keep getting this picture of the house we used to live in. I can hear all the noise and yelling inside. She wants it to stop."

It was apparent that we would not be able to continue until the part released the noise that was so distracting her. I asked Lydia to create a sizable container, and she projected a dumpster into the space in front of our chairs. As we guided the part through the release the family quarrels seeped into the dumpster like so much sewage, gradually filling it to the brim.

"I'm also hearing the arguments at work," said Lydia.

She enlarged the dumpster and put those in too, along with the sound of Mother's scolding as the little girl crouched under the stairs.

"How does the part feel now, with the noise out there instead of inside?"

"She just heaved a huge sigh of relief."

"So she finally has some real peace and quiet," I said. "But getting free of the noise is only part of it. There's also her habit of turning into an immovable rock. Ask her how she learned to do that."

"That's how Mom did it."

"Oh! And how does she benefit from becoming a rock, like Mom did?"

"It's to avoid being imposed on. But it's not a connected peace—it's a disconnected quiet."

"What is the sound of that disconnected quiet?"

"Just breathing. There's a sense of isolation."

I asked the part to look around in the isolated quiet.

"Look at all the impositions that you've been trying to avoid or disconnect from."

"I feel as if the world has been placed on my head," said Lydia, closer to tears than I'd yet seen her. "And I have glimpses of 'do this, do that, go there, do it this way.' Right up until I got sick everybody wanted a piece of me — and pieces of me were going."

"Knowing what you know now, could that have been prevented?"

"Yes. It's simply a case of setting up boundaries. I didn't know until recently that it could be done."

"How many parts of you have worlds placed on their heads?"

"Lots."

"Why not ask anyone with a world on its head to put it out in the dumpster now."

"Gladly," said Lydia.

I could well understand the rage part's dilemma. If you grow up in a large, noisy family where personal boundaries are not respected, isolating yourself can seem like an appealing solution. Likewise, a build-up of rage is a logical result of not being listened to and having to put your own needs last. That it was possible to create personal boundaries, say no to someone's request or take time for quiet reflection — these were still fairly new concepts for Lydia. She was having to painstakingly teach herself these things and learn to put them into practice. I suggested that she share these concepts with her part.

"She's amazed. She didn't know any of that was possible."

I realized that the rage part had a lot to think about, and decided to leave her to reflect while I turned my attention to the organizer — the nervous part that wanted Lydia to get a job.

"Has that part been listening in?"

"Yes. She's right here."

"What does she feel about the rage part now that she's revealed as a ten-year-old?"

"She likes her better this way—she's not so intimidating."

I asked the organizer to take a good look at Lydia's history—the long illness preceded by the years of hard work and self-denial.

"Did you contribute anything to these events?" I asked her.

"She's looking at her hands and feeling guilty," said Lydia.

"What does she feel guilty about?"

"She says she made me afraid of stopping."

"And yet you have stopped. So what has she been doing all this time that you've been sick?"

"She's been absolutely frustrated, just climbing the walls."

"I'm not surprised. She told us earlier that she considered you worthless if you were not contributing. Ask her where she got this idea."

The part recalled a scene from Lydia's childhood. Her father and older brother were building something. Little Lydia, a toddler, came forward to join in.

"They just lifted me up and moved me out of the way. As if I were an inanimate object—a chair or a lamp."

"What did the part decide?"

"That she had nothing to offer."

Other similar incidents followed and the part grew wary of being pushed aside, laughed at or made to feel useless. It became her habit to look at the world with suspicion, expecting to be devalued.

"What did she decide to do about it?"

"Try harder."

It was she who had driven Lydia to work longer hours, take on extra work and enroll in night courses.

"I did this without ever stopping to ask myself if it was what I wanted," Lydia reflected. "I was aware, of course, that my other interests had been shelved—in particular my interest in acting.

But I always imagined that this was temporary, that sometime soon I'd get back to it."

"Ask the organizer to look again at the feelings of self-worth that have been growing inside you. What does she think of them now?"

"She'd like to feel that way too."

We invited the part to share in the good energy that Lydia had been integrating over the past few years—not just the self-worth but the joy, the freedom to choose and the growing trust in her own decisions.

"Feels nice," Lydia murmured. "She could learn to like this."

Checking back with the rage part we found her feeling more peaceful and connected, though she did express a lingering fear that people might try to manipulate her.

"How does she perceive that people manipulate?"

"They tell sob stories."

"Ask her why anyone would want to manipulate her."

"To get attention."

"What does attention mean?"

"Love."

"So what people really want is love?"

"Yes."

"Ask the part: What do you know about love?"

"She's standing there feeling love all around her."

"What does love feel like to her?"

"It's like an explosion of herself outwards."

"Wow! So if people want that love, they don't need to manipulate to get it."

"It's free." She shrugged, as if to literally shuck off the mantle of perceived manipulation. I was beginning to get used to the way Lydia's mind could morph negatives into positives in the blink of an eye. I was also enjoying her highly visual, lateral way of processing, especially as it contrasted so sharply with the logical and well-organized nature of her rational mind.

There was just one question left to attend to.

"Can this part get the peace and quiet she needs without being sick?"

"Yes."

"Is she willing to be guided by what Lydia wants?"

"Yes, definitely."

I asked the two parts, the former rage part (now the love part) and the organizer, to focus on the new harmony they felt, and tell us how far back in time that went.

"All the way back to birth."

"Ask them to send the good energy they're feeling now back to themselves at birth. Clear the pathway between then and now, so that in your subconscious there's a record of this wholeness, of these parts working with you in healthy partnership."

Thus reinstated as functional, supportive parts of Lydia, they agreed to contribute what they could to the restoration of her health. We checked for doubters and objectors and found none. Everyone seemed comfortable with the new status quo.

I thought the session had been a good one. Our previous work had revolved around the use of illness as an escape, whereas this time we had brought out some entirely new dynamics — a strategy of disconnecting to get peace and quiet and a tendency to try harder to cope with feelings of worthlessness — both connected to Lydia's illness. I felt that we had delved much deeper than ever before.

We booked another appointment for a month hence. This would allow time for the parts to settle into their new roles, for Lydia to observe results and for any imbalances we may have created to make themselves known. As it turned out, the very day after the session Lydia called to say that she had come down with a painful case of shingles. A month later she was still sick and couldn't make it to our scheduled appointment.

I admit I was dismayed by this turn of events. Looking back at my case notes I find such remarks as: "I'm not sure what's going on" and "I am seriously wondering if something in Lydia does not really want her to get well." It also crossed my mind that we may have dealt insufficiently with the rage that had reared up so forcibly. Maybe the shingles was a sign of still-lingering rage working its way out through the body. Clearing out the noise, which had been aggravating the rage, may have taken the salt from the wound, but perhaps the wound itself had not actually been closed. I have often observed that unresolved rage can wreak havoc on the health.

I didn't dwell on these speculations, realizing that nothing could be confirmed until I checked with Lydia's parts. But I did feel rather glum. Had I known how close we were to the completion of our work, I might have remembered that we sometimes get worse before we get better. As our inner environment changes our parts occasionally make last-ditch attempts to pull us back into our old ways. The ghosts of old patterns and coping mechanisms tend to linger, but as we grow stronger and more integrated these increasingly lose their influence.

It was two-and-a-half months before Lydia was well enough to come for a session. As we exchanged a hug in greeting I noticed how pale and tired she looked, and so took care to handle her gently. Even before we were in our seats we began to speculate about the shingles.

I said, "I think there's still some suspicion that if you get well you're going to go straight back to your former way of life, to the exclusion of your own self. I get the feeling that concern it is not yet completely answered."

Lydia agreed, saying that even now, as she got healthier, there were more and more demands on her time. And it was always her own needs that got set aside—her morning walk, for instance, which she considered essential to her health.

"That time is mine and I want it to be non-negotiable. But I still find myself giving it up when my day gets too crowded."

In her childhood home, she reminded me, personal needs and private pleasures were not even on the map. "I was taught that time for me was totally frivolous and unimportant. Everybody else was always more important all the time than I was."

With her self-confidence growing she could trust herself to act on her own behalf most of the time. But the tendency to put her own needs last still lingered, and with it a hesitation about becoming completely well.

I knew that as she thought through this issue at a conscious level, more parts of her subconscious mind would get the message. Quite often our parts are confused simply because we ourselves fail to take a stand. There are also areas where parts actually dictate to the conscious mind. As we become more integrated, however, there is a double effect — we get more conscious and our parts become more supportive.

Our priority for this session was to look at whatever was behind Lydia's attack of shingles. We first checked in with the former rage part, but she claimed to have nothing to do with it.

"Ask inside if the changes she's made have disrupted something else."

"Yes. Another part is coming forward. It looks like a lopsided square — it's a kind of dark, brownish-green."

"What is the main feeling in the square?"

"Lack of hope."

"What effect does this lack of hope have on the physical body?"

"It weakens the immune system, leaving very little energy for repair."

The part said that after our previous session it had felt lost and confused at being left behind. This had increased its despair, further affecting the immune system. In this way, it acknowledged, it was indirectly responsible for the shingles.

"Tell the part we're sorry we left it behind. We didn't know it was there. And ask it what it believes about hope."

"It says that you have to be what you have to be."

"According to whom?"

"Everybody."

"Who is everybody?" I asked.

"I see my whole family going to visit my dad's two sisters, who lived in a small house in northern Quebec. They had very little in the way of amenities—an outdoor toilet, wood stove, no electricity."

"What did the part learn from your aunts?"

"That life is a struggle. That persistence in the face of all odds is the only way to survive." She paused, and then added, "The part is changing color to a horrible mustard yellow."

"What did persistence mean to these aunts?"

"To physically continue and to pass on what you know and what you have learned."

"What did they pass on to you?"

"Priests have power. Catholicism will win out."

"What do you believe Catholicism is?"

Lydia looked at me mutely. After a minute she shook her head and said the part was afraid of saying the wrong thing, afraid of being punished.

From a young age, she explained, she had been taught never to ask questions about religion. When she was five her mother had spanked her for asking if the baby Jesus had a brother. "The part thinks Lydia will be punished for even remembering any of this."

We thanked the part for its admissions and assured it that no one was going to punish it. "Has it been afraid to this degree all along?" I asked.

"Yes."

"Is it aware that Lydia is no longer a Catholic? Has it heard the stirrings of another belief system in Lydia?"

"Yes."

"How has that affected it?"

"It started to hope. It saw that as a lifeline but at the same time feared that it was just a trick—that if it took the lifeline it would be punished."

"Where did the part learn that a lifeline could be a trick?"

"The part learned it from my father, as I did."

She explained that, as a girl, whenever she talked back to her father, he'd let it go so far before slapping her. As she got older he allowed her to go on longer because he wanted to know what she was thinking.

"So he'd give you enough rope to hang yourself."

"Exactly."

"Were your disagreements about religion?"

"Heavens, no! We never discussed religion at home. My family said the rosary every night on their knees. Everybody had to attend and everybody said the rosary. You'd have needed a papal dispensation not to be there."

"Does the square part know that Lydia no longer lives with her family?"

"No."

We offered the part an update, informing it that Lydia's father had died and that she saw her other family members infrequently.

"Assure the part that this is not a lifeline we're throwing it. We're just telling it the truth."

The part accepted the news with relief, as indicated by a further change in its appearance. It now became three-dimensional and turned a bright, translucent green. "It looks like a cube of lime Jell-O," said Lydia.

When I asked the cube what function it performed, it told us that it lived in the abdomen, where its job was to "clear and strengthen the blood, lymph and muscles."

I was alarmed to learn that this was a body-function part, given the fear and despair it was harboring. I asked what its effect had actually been in the grand scheme of the body.

"Lack of exercise," said Lydia. "Exercise is too difficult."

"How has the part made exercise difficult?"

"Hip pain."

"Oh. Does it cause hip pain?"

"Yes, it does. I'm seeing the part contracting the muscles in this one hip." She touched her right side. "This is the hip that gives me trouble."

"Hmm. Well, it told us earlier that its job was to clear and strengthen. How does contracting the hip muscles contribute to that?"

"It says that by contracting the muscles it's creating a lymphatic pump."

"Where did it learn that?" I asked.

Lydia shook her head. "Don't know."

"Does it work? Does squeezing the muscles in that hip make the lymphatics move better?"

"Well, if I were to open and close my fist, I suppose that would work the lymphatics in my hand," she replied, demonstrating.

"Well, yes, that's a kind of pulsing. Has the part been pulsing the muscles in the hip?"

Lydia frowned. "Don't know."

"Ask it."

"No. It was just tightening them."

"Is it aware that it has not been causing the muscles to pulse, that it's just gripping."

"No, it was intended to be clearing." Lydia turned up her palms and shrugged, disclaiming all responsibility for her part's ignorance.

I asked the part to take a tour through Lydia's body and investigate just how much of this so-called clearing it had actually been doing. This was education in its most direct form. After a few minutes of scouting, the part realized that it had been focusing on just one small area of a complex system. On further investigation it came across two "filters" in Lydia's brain, though it denied having put them there. Who had put the filters in place was a bit of a puzzle. Lydia asked around amongst her parts until someone finally stepped forward out of the crowd.

"We've worked with this part before," said Lydia.

She explained that it was her joy part, formerly her disease part—the one that had removed the gauze pieces from her brain.

"She put the filters there years ago, while I was still at my job."

"What was the purpose of these filters?"

"They were intended to keep energy in."

"And have they done that?"

"No. The part sees now that all they've been doing is preventing the absorption of energy into the body."

"How many filters are there altogether?"

"It's not sure. It's been working its way through and as it finds them it clears them out."

I asked the joy part to step back so it could see all the filters at once. It found nine in total.

"Can it tell us the location of each one?"

"There are the two in the brain, one in the left forearm, one in the top left thigh, one in the right shoulder, one in the right ankle, and three in the solar plexus."

I asked the part to look at each individual filter and identify the thought or belief that was holding it in place. Starting in the brain and moving down the left side of the body, it listed the following beliefs: *I don't deserve love … I don't deserve to be healthy … I'm too tired to care … I can't be any thinner.* In the right ankle it found *exercise is difficult.* Then, *I'm not able to change,* which was in the right shoulder. Finally, it looked at the three filters in the solar plexus. *I have no right to hit my dad* was in the lower one. In the middle it identified *God's gonna get me.*

"And in the top one?"

"*Somebody else will look after me.*"

"Where did the part learn that?"

"From Catholicism. I was taught to give my power to someone else."

The whole group of beliefs was related to Catholicism, Lydia said.

Although we had worked with this part before, it was understandable that the filters had been overlooked since we had not touched on Lydia's religious beliefs. Because Lydia had consciously moved away from her Catholic upbringing, it had taken this long for these aspects of it to surface in her parts.

As I took the two parts—the cube and the joy part—through a psychic-emotive release, Lydia began to chuckle. "They're like two versions of Atlas holding up the world, staggering over to the bin with their Catholic beliefs," she said.

She also reported that they were morphing before her eyes into twelve-year-old girls. The joy part became "a curious child in a yellow dress," while the cube appeared as "an athlete in a blue track suit."

I asked both parts to do a final check of the entire body. I wanted to be sure that the lack of hope was entirely cleared out and that there were no more filters or other mechanisms that might disrupt the flow of energy. They went off hand-in-hand to see what they could find. All was well with the body, they reported, but they had come across another girl their own age, standing alone in a white dress and veil.

"She was hiding. She doesn't want to give up the dress and veil."

Lydia recognized these as the clothes she had worn to make her first communion.

"They mean a lot to her."

"What, specifically, do they mean?"

"That God loves her."

"How does she see God?"

"Like something bright that's attached to the top of her head. It's an energy that hugs her and plays with her. She's laughing and feeling loved."

"Ask her to follow that energy and see where it comes from."

"She's looking through a doorway."

"What is beyond the doorway?"

"Just a place."

"Ask her, what is this place to her."

"This is heaven!"

"Would she like to go through the doorway?"

"Yes."

Stepping across the threshold, the girl found herself in a sunny meadow filled with flowers and butterflies. Once there, she skipped out of her dress and veil, leaving them behind her in the grass.

"She feels a lot more free without them," said Lydia. "She can run around and play and lie down in the grass."

"Without her dress and veil, does God still love her?"

"Of course. She's in heaven."

Addressing Lydia's conscious mind I said, "Why not walk into that meadow and bring the other parts along."

"She's welcoming us."

"Does she know that you love her?"

"I just told her."

"Does she want to stay in this place or would she like to come home and be part of Lydia?"

"She wants to come home."

"Tell her she can bring heaven with her—and I'd like you to praise her for making it such a neat place. Given what she'd been taught, that was a very ingenious thing to do. She's quite the optimist."

We now had three parts, all of them twelve-year-old girls, a happy trio. When I asked them if they wanted to grow up, they answered with a resounding yes.

"If they could grow up just as they'd like to, without any rules or oppression, how would they turn out?" I asked.

In answer they burst into a peal of giggles.

I invited them to join hands and drift back in time until they could see who they were and what they were doing before they began to close off energy. In that original state, they discovered, they were energetic and fun-loving. They held such beliefs as: *good health is a natural state … hope is normal … I'm free to express myself … I'm worthy … I'm part of God … I trust myself.*

"Ask them to look at Lydia's life, at how it gradually shut down, at how they and many other parts never grew up. What do they think about that from where they are now?"

"It was unnecessary."

"Can they see what the lesson is?"

"The bottom line is to continue to trust myself."

"What do they know now that would allow Lydia to be more confident about protecting her own space and time?"

"She's worth it."

"It makes sense."

"I am worth it," said Lydia.

I asked her to explain to her parts what our basic contract had been throughout all of her processes. She wanted to be healthy yet still at liberty to choose her own path, in spite of other people's expectations. At the same time, if she should decide to respond to some demand or request, she was free to do so. It was entirely up to her.

"Can they support you in this?"

"Yes."

"We want to see you healthy, strong and full of reliable energy. Energy that you can count on. And it's up to you consciously to do whatever you like with that energy, including being lazy if that's what you want. How do the parts feel about that? Is it possible?"

"Yes."

I asked them to begin bringing their energy forward through time, and as they came forward, to let go of their old restrictive beliefs. Reading from my notes, I gave them some prompts.

"Dissolve the beliefs that *if I ask questions I'll be punished* ... that *life itself is a struggle* ... that *a lifeline can be a trick* ... that *I must persist in the face of all odds* and that *I must create odds to persist against*. Dissolve any belief that *there's no hope* ... that *I have to give away my power* ... that *I have to put other people ahead of myself* ... and that *the only way I can get free of my obligations is to be sick*. Dissolve the belief that *someone else will take care of me*. Dissolve the whole link to illness."

When the parts arrived in the present, Lydia opened her eyes and looked at me. Her gaze seemed darker and deeper than ever. When I asked her how she felt, she said, "tired but relaxed."

Thus ended our work on Lydia's illness.

As I reflected on the session over the next few days, it seemed to me that the Jell-O cube, by suppressing the immune system, had likely played a major role in the ME. In fact, it was a wonder that Lydia had made any progress at all, given the part's lack of hope and its belief that any potential lifeline is a trick.

About three months later I gave Lydia a call to see how she was doing. This is what she told me:

On arriving home from the session she had rested for a day or two. Then, her energy had picked up in a big way. She was out walking nearly every day, doing four kilometers at a stretch. She felt tired afterwards but not wiped out. She noted the absence of exhaustion and other symptoms like swollen glands. Meanwhile, her mind and perception had also improved—she found it easier to make decisions and to act on her own behalf. Overall, on that zero-to-ten scale we'd been using, she placed herself well above her previous level of four. On bad days she might drop as low as seven, whereas on good days she was up to nine.

This leap in well being had occurred over just three months, the period of our three final sessions. The vitality and good humor in her voice were delightful to hear and provided additional testimony to her renewed health.

We've kept in touch in the intervening six years and Lydia has reported no relapses. In the first two years following our work she learned that she could count on her energy and began expanding her range of activities. I remember her calling one day during that period to invite me to lunch. When I put down the phone I felt slightly stunned—I could still hear her telling me at our first meeting how tired it made her to chew and digest food. Currently, she reports that her energy has not returned to the level it was at before her illness, but she is able to live a normal life. That includes working at things she enjoys and going dancing with her husband on a regular basis.

I always ask the question, what are the benefits of this illness, or in other words, what are you gaining by going through it? So often we create illness as a way of breaking out of a rut or changing our life path, as was true of Lydia. Unlike many others, however, Lydia recognized and accepted this from the start. She was far more willing than most to assume responsibility for her misfortunes, and indeed for everything that happened to her in life. This—coupled with her belief that it was actually possible to get well—virtually assured the success of our work.

An equally important asset was her strong belief in the link between her psychological and physical well being. She never doubted that if she improved the one, the other would follow. This fueled her persistence and gave her a significant edge. When we don't believe that we can heal, the process is usually much more difficult. The mind leads and inspires the physical body.

During the time I worked with Lydia I learned to understand

and respect the way she paced herself. She told me once that during the first year of her illness she had tried to will herself past her symptoms—but the more she pushed the sicker she got. Only when she relaxed and began to accept her limitations did she start to improve. Generally speaking, those afflicted by tired diseases have done far too much forcing and pushing—the lesson is in backing off and being more accepting of inner needs and rhythms. Lydia is a perfect case in point: Her recovery was a process of learning self-respect. The key question for Lydia was and will be: How do I enjoy good health and still remain true to myself?

The Hunger

Shannon had consulted me from time to time over the years and I'd always enjoyed working with her. She was quick on the uptake, liked to laugh and zoomed through her processes quickly and efficiently, usually getting excellent results. One summer day when I hadn't seen her for a couple of years, she called for an appointment.

"There's something I need your help with," she said. "I'll tell you when I see you."

The morning of our appointment rolled around warm and sunny, and Shannon showed up in skin-tight biking shorts and tank top—black and lime green. I thought she looked fit and striking. Her curly red hair was becomingly disheveled and her hazel eyes were bright.

"Here's the problem," she said as we took our seats. "My sugar addiction has gone right out of control. I've been gaining weight and if it doesn't stop I'll be as big as a house."

I found this mildly surprising since I'd worked with Shannon many times and she had never before mentioned a sugar addiction. Any given process usually touches on a wide range of issues, so it isn't often that something stays completely hidden.

I asked for a few pertinent details. She'd had a sweet tooth as a child, she said, which she considered normal. Then, some eight years ago, during her brief marriage to Tim, a fitness instructor, it had turned into a full-blown sugar addiction.

"That's when I started being a secret eater. I used to hide food

201

and when Tim wasn't around I'd pig out. It was really important to him that I stay thin and so he came down on me if I ate anything extra."

I did recall her mentioning in the past that Tim had nagged her about her weight. And I could see that she had gained a few pounds, though she was by no means fat.

"So guess what?" she continued. "Even after we broke up and I had my own place, I was still hiding food. It was ridiculous because I lived by myself."

We laughed.

"What kind of food were you hiding?" I asked.

"At the time it was probably anything forbidden—cookies, donuts, candy. I wasn't hiding apples."

But these days, she said, she was into chocolate bars—and had taken to keeping a stash of them in her night table. Over the past few months she had found herself scarfing them down in the night when she was barely conscious. She only realized she was doing this because she was finding empty wrappers on the floor beside her bed.

"I see the wrapper, and then I vaguely remember waking up in the night and eating the candy bar."

She was also indulging during the day. Most recently, she had polished off a box of chocolates that she'd intended to give as a gift. She was awake at the time but powerless to stop herself. That was the incident that had prompted her to call me.

I asked her to think about what might be triggering these sugar binges. Could she pin it down to a particular emotion, like boredom or frustration?

More likely it was the sheer intensity of her life, she said. "I'll have a really full day at work, and then race off to an evening class. I'll come home, do a few chores and fall into bed around midnight. That might be a night when I'd get up and eat a candy bar without really knowing about it."

She ate well during the day, she said, and wasn't hungry when she got home. Nor was she fatigued. No matter how busy she got, she explained, she always took time to relax on weekends. On the whole she found life exciting and fulfilling and was happier than she'd ever been. In short, there was no obvious reason for the binges.

What she wanted from our session was not to give up eating candy altogether but to put it in balance. "We need to work with the sugar gremlin," she said. "The part that's just gotta have it, that can't say no."

I agreed that would be a good place to start. And because we had worked together often I began without further discussion.

"I'd like you to ask inside if that sugar-eating part of you, the one that gets up in the night and eats candy bars, would be willing to communicate."

After a pause, she said, "I'm getting a slightly nauseous feeling. The words that come to mind are: I don't want to do this anymore." She shook her head forlornly. "He's a sad little part. He doesn't have a lot of hope that he can change."

"I can understand that," I sympathized.

"This part is definitely a he," she added. "I'm getting a very masculine feeling."

"Can the part tell you what job he does for you?" I asked.

"I'm hearing the words: Gobble up the world. That's what the part is doing."

"Can he tell you what he's trying to accomplish for you by gobbling up the world?"

"He can see that I want a lot out of life. He wants to encourage me and he wants to show his solidarity."

"Ask the part how he does that."

"When I take on something new or try to go forward there's sometimes doubt: Can I do this? By woofing down a candy bar the part is telling me that I can do it."

At that moment she started to squirm violently in her chair. "I'm getting this terrible itching in my genital area," she gasped.

"Would you like to put socks on your hands?" I asked straight-faced.

She stared at me for an instant before we both burst out laughing. The joke went back a long way—Shannon had complained of genital itching from the first time we'd worked together. The itching was caused by a bumpy rash that tended to develop on her thighs and outer labia. A couple of times in the past we had worked on it directly. Each time we worked it subsided for a while and then reappeared. And with each reappearance, a different part claimed to be in charge of it. I have run into other cases where different parts take over a given symptom, each for its own reasons. I hoped we would eventually be able to heal the rash entirely, but for now it was at least providing a way for different parts to call attention to themselves. Not that this was any immediate comfort to Shannon, who was now out of her chair and pacing the room in discomfort.

"You'll have to excuse me," she said. Turning her back, she gave herself a scratch and then hobbled back to her chair.

"Is there something the itching wants to say?" I asked.

"The phrase I'm getting now is: itching to get out there. The part is literally itching to get out in the world. There's a sense of urgency here. I can't do enough things fast enough. I can't eat the candy bar fast enough. I'm itching to get on with it."

This part, as we discovered, was all anticipation and excitement. It gave Shannon a big, powerful feeling. Not scary, she said, but sometimes overwhelming. I asked this anticipation part about its relationship to the sugar part.

"It's simple," she said. "If anticipation isn't gratified the poor little sugar gremlin has to eat something."

The sugar part was not only providing gratification, he was also giving the anticipation part fuel, which it accepted as motivation to keep moving forward.

"What would happen if the sugar part were to stop doing his job?" I asked.

"If the sugar part stopped doing his job?" Shannon repeated thoughtfully. "The anticipation part would feel empty."

"So the anticipation part is dependent on the sugar part?"

"Not completely. I mean, it does want to be filled up. With food or — I'm even getting a sexual feeling of being literally filled during intercourse. But it also wants to accomplish things. It wants recognition. It's that empty feeling it's afraid of ..." She broke off suddenly and rolled her eyes. "Now my stomach is crawling."

"What does that mean?"

"I'm hungry."

"Is it a physical hunger?"

"Yes, but its also a representation of that empty feeling."

"What does feeling empty mean to the anticipation part?"

"That it won't get things accomplished, and so it won't feel fulfilled." She paused; then added, "This is real hunger in the largest sense of the word. A hunger to do everything. A hunger to grow."

This made sense to me. Often with eating disorders, the feeling of emptiness goes well beyond the physical level. It was also interesting that the anticipation part was positively motivated, even though it was causing troublesome behavior. It made me think of the sorcerer's apprentice getting carried away with his job.

I asked the anticipation part how old it was.

"It says thirty-six." She laughed. "I'm forty-four, so it's eight years behind me."

"Hmm. Well ask the part: What is significant to you about Shannon at age thirty-six?"

She stared into space and after a moment looked like she might start to cry. "That was when I decided to be free," she said. "And to be true to myself. I'd forgotten about that."

"Is it sad?"

"No, it's not. It was such a good feeling when I made that decision. It feels like this part of me has only recently connected with that commitment."

She thought the connection had happened about four months earlier when one day at work it dawned on her that she had been "hiding her light under a bushel." Since then, she'd been putting out more and had found that people were responding positively.

"What has happened to the anticipation part as a result of that?" I asked.

"It's gotten bigger and stronger. This is a part that was created a long time ago and never had a chance to grow. It's a really big part of me." Her eyes pooled with tears. "It's a feeling that I'm finally doing the right thing."

When she had cried a little and blown her nose she said, "There's an aspect to this part that's like a horse out of the gate." She paused, closing her eyes. "I see a beautiful chestnut horse—a mare. She's trotting around a corral."

"How does she feel being in that corral?"

"It's a choice. She could leap over the fence if she wanted to."

"What would determine if she leapt over?"

"If she wanted to do different things than she's doing right now. The corral is what she's doing right now because she knows she can't take on the whole planet."

"So it's a choice. But even though she's choosing it, what is she feeling as she's trotting around the corral?"

Shannon acknowledged that the mare felt a little constrained— but insisted that she actually wanted to be corralled. And yet, while Shannon didn't see it as a problem, I was concerned about the confinement of this brimming energy. I asked the mare if she knew who had put the fence there or who was in charge of it.

"The mare herself is in charge of the fence," said Shannon.

"Has Shannon had any input into this?"

She hesitated, and then shook her head.

"Ask the mare: How old do you think Shannon is?"

Shannon blinked. "She says thirty-four."

This was interesting, not only because Shannon was actually forty-four, but because the anticipation part—of which the mare was an aspect—had told us a few moments earlier that its own age was thirty-six.

"So what is it about Shannon at age thirty-four that's significant to you?" I asked the mare.

"She isn't ready to handle this energy. She isn't ready to handle the whole pasture, so to speak."

"What do you believe makes her unable to handle the whole pasture?"

"Too much self-doubt."

"So you've corralled yourself."

"That's right. Because of my energy. It's too much for her."

"Hmm. Well Shannon, maybe we should let this mare in on the secret that you are now forty-four. What do you think?"

"Good idea."

"I'll tell you what. I want you, forty-four-year-old Shannon, to go sit on the fence and introduce yourself to the mare."

She gazed into the near distance. "The mare just stopped in her tracks and looked at me. She's knows who I am. She's coming over." She laughed. "This is just like watching a movie."

"How do you feel about her?"

"Affectionate. I'm rubbing her nose and feeding her sugar lumps."

"Ask this part to take a good look at you—to see how ready you are to handle this energy."

"She thinks I could handle it."

"Okay, good. Now ask her to apply some X-ray vision to that fence. What are some of the thoughts that make up its structure?"

Without hesitation Shannon replied, "*You can't do this … Life doesn't work that way … What makes you think you can achieve this?"*

"Ask the mare: Do you agree with those thoughts?"

"No. She really hates those ideas."

"Where did they come from?"

"Mom. It sounds just like her."

"Okay. I'm wondering if any of this fence belongs to Shannon."

"No."

"So ask the mare: What thoughts or feelings do you hold that have allowed it to exist?"

Shannon shut her eyes tight. "Self-doubt," she said. "The phrase that comes to mind is: Can I do this?"

I reminded her of our earlier discovery that this exact phrase—Can I do this?—was what triggered the sugar gremlin to go into action. It seemed there was a domino effect going on. When self-doubt came into play, the anticipation part was corralled and the sugar gremlin woofed down a candy bar, which filled the emptiness and fueled forward movement.

"So let's look at the main belief under the self-doubt," I suggested.

She lowered her eyes. "I'm not worthy."

"Not worthy of what?"

"Not worthy to receive this."

"What is *this*?"

Her face crumpled with emotion. "It's like … abundance. Everything that is good. Everything that feels wonderful."

"How old was Shannon when she decided that she wasn't worthy to receive abundance?"

She answered in a tiny voice. "I feel about three years old."

I asked the mare what had precipitated the decision.

"Something about feelings in the body. The things that felt good, like eating and drinking out of a bottle."

"How did we feel about those body feelings?"

"They felt wonderful."

"And what happened then?"

She frowned. "Something got taken away. I don't know what."

"Allow the part to take its time. And ask it: What was taken away?"

Her eyes flew open. "It was the right—the right to feel good. It wasn't anything that was done to me, it was a judgment: Nobody should be that joyful. Nobody should feel that good."

"Ah. Whose judgment was that?"

"Mom's." She shook her head, exasperated.

"You may have been overwhelming to her in some ways," I suggested.

"I'm sure I was. They've told me that as a little kid I was just unbridled. Less so as I got older. I must have taken her judgment to heart."

I was all too familiar with the phenomenon of repressed enthusiasm. About three years earlier I had discovered a part of myself that had literally frozen in the act of jumping for joy. Kids are always being told to tone it down, which is understandable, but it's not good to get into the habit of suppressing our positive energy. When we suppress any natural expression it inevitably comes out in some way, quite often as a troublesome symptom or behavior—like Shannon's sugar binges.

Shannon's mother had also taught her that "good feelings don't last" and that "you'll be disappointed in the end." I knew from previous work with Shannon that her mother had been subject to depression. We had already dealt with much of the programming Shannon had picked up living with a depressed mother, but the judgment on her right to feel good was a new twist, and even as she identified it she was gripped by self-doubt.

"It's been this way for so long, I don't see how it can change."

Given the mare's self doubt—it felt so inhibited as to actually corral itself—I thought it was natural for Shannon to experience self-doubt as she worked with it. When you probe into a part's feelings, those feelings well up in you—not a bad thing since it provides an opportunity to examine and release them. And, in fact, when I asked the mare if she could separate Mom's judgment from her own abundant energy, she did so with a sigh of relief.

"The fence has collapsed," said Shannon. "It's just a bunch of rails lying on the ground."

The mare stepped over the rails into the larger pasture, but still, she was not ready to gallop off in search of adventure. She looked at Shannon and whinnied softly, telling her that she was worried.

"Life is a struggle. It's haphazard and unpredictable. You don't know what will happen, how things will turn out." It was the part speaking, but these were worries that Shannon recognized.

"When you say you don't know what will happen, you're talking about outside things," I said. "But we're talking about inside things right now. And it's only inside things we can really be sure of."

This caught her interest.

"Has Shannon's love for herself lasted?" I asked.

"Yes."

"Has Shannon's love for people lasted?"

"Yes."

"And for life?"

"Yes."

"Has her enthusiasm been scotched forever by any external event?"

"No. It's never been extinguished. It's been put under bushels and circumscribed by fences but it's always survived."

"Is that predictable then?"

"Yes."

"Is Shannon's basic nature predictable?"

"Yes."

"Does the part agree with all of this?"

"Yes. She's saying: I can count on Shannon."

"That's the one thing you *can* count on. The only thing that's predictable is our center, our commitment to ourselves. As Shannon gets stronger and more confident she'll be able to create external events in ways that are more predictable — but an element of unpredictability will always remain. That's part of the excitement and the challenge, part of negotiating life."

"The mare has become very contemplative. She needed to hear that she could count on Shannon. That really makes a difference to her."

"Let her contemplate that for a while. And let me know when she's ready to throw the fence rails out."

"They're already gone. That feels much better."

"Good. I'd like you to thank her — and ask her if she can be patient while we check on the sugar gremlin."

"He wants to know where he fits in."

"That's an important question, and we're about to find out. Let's ask this sugar part: How old was Shannon when you were first created."

"Thirty-three or thirty-four."

"So that was ten years go. What decision did we make at that age?"

"Wanting to gobble up life. Wanting to take on more — do more and be more."

"Does the part understand the difference between physical food as fuel and other kinds of energy, like joy or enthusiasm, which are also fuel?"

She took a moment to reply. "Yes. But he says food fuel was the only fuel Shannon would accept."

"Was there a part of Shannon that couldn't accept anything but food fuel?"

"My stomach," she said uncertainly. "I'm getting this empty feeling in my stomach."

The stomach had been grumbling in the background ever since

the session began—it was time we found out what it was up to. In answer to my questions the stomach said that it did know the difference between food fuel and other kinds of fuel—that it had always known the difference but had made an agreement with the sugar gremlin.

"Ask your stomach: What did you agree to?"

"This is unbelievable," said Shannon. "It agreed to be a conduit so the sugar gremlin could provide energy for the anticipation part. The stomach agreed even though it knew that it wasn't sugar that was really needed."

"So the stomach knew. And the sugar part knew. The anticipation part is the one that was not making the distinction—it was confusing physical and emotional fuel as well as physical and emotional emptiness."

"That's right. And the stomach doesn't really like the sugar but it's been going along for the sake of satisfying the anticipation part. It's a go-between."

"How does it feel about being a go-between?"

"It doesn't want to do it anymore."

"Does it know that it doesn't have to?"

She shut her eyes. "The anticipation part is telling the stomach that it's over. And you know what? The stomach is thanking it."

"So let's ask the anticipation part: What fuel does it really need?"

"Shannon's commitment. Realizing that it can count on me has assured it that it doesn't need to use the stomach anymore."

"Make sure everybody has a good understanding that the stomach is now relieved of that job," I said. "And let the sugar part know that he can retire."

Shannon nodded.

"Would he like a gold watch?" I asked dryly.

Shannon laughed and said, "Why not?" But a moment later she remarked, "The sugar part is gone."

"Gone?"

"He disappeared into the stomach. He's not there anymore."

"Is his essence there?"

"No. He wasn't a real part. He was just—how can I put it—a representation of the link between physical and non-physical fuel."

Parts don't often disappear and it took me a moment to register. I must have looked puzzled.

"Sorry," she said. "It's hard to explain."

"I think I understand. Has the sugar part been fully reabsorbed by the stomach?"

"Yes. He was just a product of the agreement."

"He was just a little minion."

"That's right. He was a servant whose job was to eat. I felt so sorry for him."

"Interesting. Let's go back to the anticipation part for a moment—along with its horse-out-of-the-gate feeling. How does it feel about this turn of events?"

She closed her eyes to concentrate. "It's relieved that it doesn't have to organize these kinds of agreements anymore. It was so much work just to get that little bit of energy."

"Is there any other fuel it needs now besides Shannon's commitment? Because it did have a list earlier—it wanted to be sexually filled, it wanted recognition …"

"It feels satisfied because I've recognized it."

"There was also its hunger to do and be everything. Which was the state of mind that went with feeling trapped and unable to free the energies."

"I don't have that feeling anymore."

"Does it have any hunger at all?"

"No. It just feels full of confidence in me."

"And how does it feel now about receiving life's abundance?"

"It just flows in."

"Ask the part: Can you accept life's abundance?"

"Yes. It says: I can accept life's abundance. I accept it and I deserve it."

"And you're worthy of it."

"I am worthy of it. It feels so good." She laughed. "The part isn't a horse anymore—it's a column of light that runs right through me." She gestured from her feet to the top of her head. "But don't we have to go back in time?" she asked.

As someone who had worked with me previously she was accustomed to the textbook rollover, where the parts find a base in the past. But Shannon's part had spontaneously uncovered its link to her core in the present.

"We don't need to," I said.

"How come?"

I shrugged. "It's all here, where you're at."

"You mean it's already here."

"That's right."

"Wow!" she said. "I don't have to go back. It's right here."

"There is one thing I'd like to check, though. I'm wondering what is more important to you: Recognition from others or your own recognition of yourself. I'd like you and all your parts to think about that."

She didn't hesitate. "I think that being true to myself can give me far more satisfaction than I could ever get being told that I did a good job."

"Make sure all your parts hear that. *I recognize me.*"

"*I recognize me.* I do. This is gonna be a great meditation."

On this positive note, the session came to an end.

It was nearly a year later when I finally sent Shannon an e-mail, inquiring how things had worked out. She answered within hours, reporting that her sugar craving had disappeared the day of our session, never to return. The promise of abundance had also come true, she reported. In the months since I'd seen her she had graduated from university, been promoted at work, bought a house, and was considering the offer of another promotion that would mean moving to New York. Here is what she wrote:

"Sometimes I feel the need to come and see you so we can tweak parts, but I have such a great inner foundation that everything just flows for me. I know that all the abundance and love in my life have come through the work we've done together."

———————————

Shannon's session was so straightforward partly because she and I had worked together many times before. As a result of that work her conscious clarity had grown and her parts had become more spontaneous in their responses.

Looking back at the logic of things, I would say that her sugar addiction hinged primarily on the decision she had made at age thirty-six — to be free and true to herself. In deciding that, she was picking up a primary feeling of exuberance that had been stifled — a hunger to do and be everything, as exemplified by the horse-out-of-the-gate feeling. But the renewed impulse to charge ahead brought her old self-doubting beliefs into play, as illustrated by the corralled mare. The result was an emotional start-stop pattern that led to the development of a coping mechanism, namely the sugar addiction.

In my opinion, eating disorders rarely have an organic base — in fact, I've found that they are often fueled by very positive parts. For example, Pearl and Mark (see "Neverland" and "Half in Love with Easeful Death") both had positively motivated eating parts, as did Shannon. In Shannon's case there was very little to change — it was simply a matter of resolving the areas of self-doubt, and thus taking the lid off her exuberance.

It made things simpler that Shannon did not have a weight problem. While compulsive-eating patterns are often easily resolved, actual weight loss can take more time. When obesity is a factor there are often entrenched metabolic patterns in place at both the emotional and physical levels. People may unconsciously program their metabolisms to keep their bodies heavy, which provides certain benefits.

To offer an example, not long ago I worked with a woman who was seventy-five pounds overweight, although her eating patterns appeared to be normal. She told me that she had to starve herself for months to lose even a few pounds. My response was to ask her to look at the benefits of being heavy, which she did with admirable insight. To begin with, she thought she was using her weight to keep her husband in his place. She didn't feel loved or respected by him and didn't want him to get the idea that she would make herself attractive for his benefit. At another level, she harbored the belief that she had to be heavy in order to fit in with the women in her family, who were all fat. Then again, she was just so used to her size that it had become part of her identity. Looking at these issues was eye-opening for her, but she could not muster the conscious intent to begin working on them. I found it easy to sympathize as I knew that changing these factors would involve a complete metamorphosis of her personality—something that many people are not willing to undertake.

Healing can often be simpler than we think. But it does require a willingness to look deeply within ourselves, to accept growth and change, and most importantly, to open ourselves to love.

Epilogue

The story of my own anorexia and bulimia offers an interesting backdrop to the cases in this book. It also reveals the nature and substance of my professional roots. Of course, as a therapist, there is nothing like having first-hand experience of a compulsive-obsessive disorder. But more importantly, my condition impelled me to look for answers — and that ultimately led to the philosophy and techniques that inform my current practice.

I was fourteen when I first became anorexic, though I can see in retrospect that I'd been building up to it for years, as one of my earliest memories reveals. In this memory I am three years old, sitting on an elderly uncle's knee at the dinner table.

"Eat your biscuits and gravy, dear," my uncle tells me kindly. "They'll make you nice and fat." I am horror struck at the thought of getting fat and push my plate away.

When I was growing up an aversion to fat ran through my whole family, so it was inevitable that I too would pick up on it. But the clincher for me was hearing my parents' snide remarks about an aunt, who was not only obese but had spent much of her life institutionalized with mental problems. When I was still very young, the two conditions, fat and insanity, became inseparably linked in my mind.

As I grew older I became critical of the women in our small Colorado farming community, including my mother. I saw them as forever going on diets, yet never losing weight, and although many of them had been to university they were not using their minds. To me, their lives seemed utterly vacuous and I was determined that I would not grow up to be like them.

The year I turned thirteen I began to mature physically and I didn't like it. Growing up mentally was okay but I was mortified by the changes that were happening in my body. I weighed myself every day and became increasingly alarmed as the scales crept up and up, eventually reaching 107 pounds. This was heavier than I'd ever been in my life and I felt absolutely enormous. (I was actually a perfect weight for my height, though nothing would have convinced me of this at the time.)

I turned fourteen on May 23rd, 1962. That morning, I was lying on the grass in front of our house when a totally new thought entered my mind — a flash of pure inspiration that would change my life. I would simply get rid of the weight I had gained in the past year, and more. All I had to do was stop eating fattening foods. It would be easy.

From that moment on I was completely transformed. Saying nothing to anyone, I began my regimen that day and found that it took no effort at all. Everything in me obeyed. Not only did I cut down my food intake to almost nil, I began running two to three miles every morning before school. I felt hungry, but hunger was a friend — it meant that I was losing weight.

Within a month I was down to ninety pounds and thrilled with my progress. From my point of view I was getting more beautiful by the day. When I went back to school that fall I felt proud of the fact that I was not busting out all over like the other girls. While they were growing, I was shrinking. While I was on the way to perfection, they were getting fat. Some of them were already fat.

Yet even at ninety pounds I wasn't satisfied. I feared that at any moment I would lose control and start eating again. In addition there was the problem of feeling fat and seeing myself as fat. I wasn't hallucinating — I knew the difference between my internal image of myself and the physical reality. But at the same time, there was a degree of distortion going on. Looking in the mirror I'd focus on a little bulge — a bit of tissue that was not in perfect alignment with the rest of the tissue — and this filled me with dismay.

It was later that summer, during a visit to my granny in Florida, that I discovered the trick of throwing up. I don't remember exactly how the idea came to me but I do know that it was entirely my own. I hadn't read about it or heard anyone talking about it — I thought it up myself.

Granny was a feeder. She loved to cook and would have liked nothing better than to send me home to my mother with an extra ten pounds on me. At every meal she laid on great platters of all the foods that were on my strictly forbidden list, and served me extra-large portions. Of course I didn't want any of it — but I didn't always know how to refuse. One day at lunch I ate some sandwiches from a large plateful that she had put in front of me. After the meal I went into the washroom, leaned over the toilet bowl and stuck two fingers down my throat. I retched, but to my dismay nothing came up. It took a strong will and repeated tries before I actually managed to vomit. The whole experience was extremely unpleasant but I felt a lot better afterwards, and Granny was none the wiser.

Back home in Colorado I learned that it's much easier to throw up when you've got a really full stomach. I began to indulge in outrageous eating binges, relying on the fact that I could simply get rid of it afterwards. The binges became more and more habitual until eventually they were happening on a daily basis. I would consume everything I could get my hands on and I especially craved all the foods that I had cut out as an anorexic. Bologna and mayonnaise sandwiches were high on my list, as were pot pies from the family freezer. I even stole food that my mother planned to serve for dinner. It got so bad that she had locks installed on the fridge, freezer and kitchen cupboards, at which point, in desperation, I began forging her signature on checks so I could buy food at the local grocery store. When she put a stop to that as well, things got difficult but I still managed what meager binges I could.

By this time my parents knew what I was up to because in a moment of guilt I had confessed that I was throwing up "on purpose" to lose weight. Still, I resented any intrusion or interference. On occasion my mother would stand outside the washroom as I was getting rid of my dinner and call through the door, "Are you off now, Ellen?" At this I would fly into a rage and reply, "No! I'm not off!" Nobody could take it away from me.

By my fifteenth birthday I weighed only sixty-nine pounds and my parents were certain they were going to lose me. They sent me to a psychiatrist, who urged me to check myself into the local hospital for treatment. As concerned as he was, however, he was unwilling to commit me against my will and for that I was grateful. I had no intention of going into the hospital because I didn't think there was anything wrong with me. I had done this to myself and as far as I was concerned I was winning.

One night, several months before my sixteenth birthday, something changed. Lying in bed, unable to sleep, I became aware of a strange physical sensation that seemed to emanate from my very cells and tissues. It came into my mind that this was what people called malnutrition.

"If I go to sleep tonight," I thought, "I won't wake up in the morning."

I didn't want to die. It had never been my intention to kill myself and only now did I realize that I'd taken things too far. I sat up all that night. The next morning I went down to the kitchen where my mother was making breakfast and asked her to drive me to the hospital.

Over the following months I cooperated with the doctors and got my weight up to 102 pounds. The resident psychiatrist, who worked with me on a daily basis, showed real interest in me and a respect that I'd never received before. He taught me about the facts of life and awakened in me a glimmer of pride in being female. The day I was released from hospital I resumed my old bulimic habits, yet there was a difference. In order to stay alive and have normal menses, I decided to maintain my weight at ninety pounds. Through trial and error I found that I could achieve this by keeping down a quart of orange juice every day. In this way I managed to stay in reasonably good health despite my ongoing problem.

By the time I was out of my teens I was fed up with my eating disorder, but it had long since become compulsive. I consulted numerous counselors and psychiatrists to no avail; it was appallingly clear that traditional psychology had no answers for me. Like any addict, I began to promise myself each day that I would reform tomorrow. But as the years passed and nothing changed, I began to see the irony of my situation: What had started as a way to take control of my life had ended by taking control away.

Throughout my twenties I was intensely involved with searching for a cure. I became a voracious consumer of psychology texts and self-help books and as I approached my thirties I began taking courses in a range of alternate therapies. The techniques of Eriksonian hypnotherapy made the biggest impact on me. I became skilled in the practice of hypnosis and—together with an associate—operated a hypnotherapy clinic in Washington state. We helped people quit smoking and lose weight and I learned to excel at self-hypnosis (using it to anaesthetize myself in the dentist's chair and to achieve my first perfect score in archery), but a cure for my bulimia continued to elude me.

My disorder was easier to manage as an adult because I earned my own money and no longer had to steal food. Yet it continued to cause me embarrassment and distress. I recall haunting an all-you-can-eat restaurant in San Francisco, returning again and again to the buffet table as the staff looked on in disbelief. I had a recurring dream that I ate all the food at a banquet and couldn't find a place to throw up. I awoke from this dream in a panic, desperately needing to vomit when there was nothing in my stomach. By the early 1980s my bulimia had become a way of life. I was still looking for a cure but no longer had much hope that I would find one. I had started so young that I couldn't even imagine what a bulimia-free existence might be like.

Then, on a spring evening in 1982 I was visiting a friend who lived in the country outside Vancouver. He and I had taken some alternative psychology courses together, and we sometimes met to exchange ideas and improvise with techniques. In general, we liked to call on our individual backgrounds—courses we had taken or books we had read—to develop experiments that could take us in new directions. On this occasion our session involved identifying a specific feeling, and then tracking it back through time by asking the question, "Do you remember ever feeling that way before?" I took my turn as guinea pig and began with a feeling of inadequacy, which eventually wound its way back to a deep core of self-hatred. Our experiment was not directed at my bulimia—my friend had no idea that I was bulimic, and I myself had never made a connection between the bulimia and my feelings of inadequacy.

As our session progressed I followed a series of memories, each one filled with humiliation and self-loathing. When I had gone as far back as I could, my friend suggested that I challenge these feelings by saying the words, "I love me."

"Forget it," I said.

I would not even consider saying such a thing. The very idea went against everything in me. But my refusal merely fueled my friend's determination. The more I resisted the more insistent he became. We must have argued for hours, though I knew even then that my real argument was with myself. When he finally left me alone to think things over, I continued to struggle along on my own.

I spent a long time debating with myself, recalling all the bad things I'd done in my life and trying to figure out how I could love myself in spite of them. I even tried reciting the magic words in a whisper, but something in me said that this was wrong and couldn't be. It seemed to me like trying to mix oil with water—it just wasn't going to work.

Finally, my friend came back into the room to see how I was doing.

"Why not yell it out and be done with it," he suggested, exasperated.

"That's just not possible." I replied, equally frustrated.

"Well it's getting late, so if you're going to do it you'd better get on with it."

I looked at my watch and was shocked to see that it was nearing midnight. He was right—it was time for me to be going. If I wanted to make a move I had to do it now.

I got up and went outside into the clear night air. I felt no more ready for this than I had hours earlier and was tempted to leave it for another day, but now my pride was involved—I didn't want to admit defeat. At least the cabin was isolated and there were no other houses within hailing distance.

Closing my eyes I took a big breath, held it for a moment, and then bellowed out the words, "I love me," to the surrounding trees. This time, everything in me heard. It was as if with one trumpet blast all the walls came crashing down. I stood for a moment in stunned silence. After that I broke into sobs, and then, unexpectedly, came euphoria.

Driving home that night I stopped to eat in a restaurant on the highway, and when I'd finished my meal I didn't bother going to the washroom to throw up. At the time this didn't strike me as having any special significance. There had always been the odd occasion when I got distracted and skipped the usual ritual. But as the days passed and I continued to eat normally and keep everything down, the incredible truth began to dawn on me: I was no longer bulimic. Nor did I revert to anorexia as I had occasionally done in the past.

The euphoria lasted three months. It took somewhat longer for my digestion to return to normal.

As I considered and reconsidered the events of that fateful evening I began to understand that the essence of my cure had been a belief change. On some level the dynasty of "I hate me" had been overturned by the regime of "I love me." The struggle that had gone on within me that night had, in fact, been a battle of wills with my self-hatred "part."

I don't advocate trying to force new beliefs on parts. It is a brutal way to proceed, and in most cases simply doesn't work. That the new belief actually took hold on that occasion I consider to be something of a miracle. But take hold it did. Although I have since tangled with other self-negating aspects of myself, that one part has always remained strong and true. What never ceases to amaze me is how devoted parts become to their new jobs, once they decide to make a change.

Acknowledgements

Thanks go first to all those whose stories appear here, for being adventurous and trusting enough to try a novel approach to solving their physical problems, and for their willingness to share their experience.

Diane Scally, Michael Blake Read, John Massey and Richard Thibodeau deserve much gratitude for their ongoing support and encouragement.

We would also like to acknowledge Beth Kapusta for her professional input; Patrick Crean and Beth Crane for sharing their expertise; and Frances Hanna for believing in the book.

Last but not least, we appreciate all those friends and colleagues who read the work-in-progress and offered suggestions.

p97 0M

Elly Roselle has devoted her career to exploring the dynamics of change in the human psyche. Her unique methodology, Core Belief Engineering, was sparked by the cure of her own anorexia and bulimia in 1982, and has evolved through two decades of independent study and work with clients. Originally from Colorado, Roselle is now based in White Rock, British Columbia. She lectures, teaches and maintains her private practice.